THE INVISIBLE GOVERNMENT

I know no safe depository of the ultimate powers of society but the people themselves; and if we think them not enlightened enough to exercise their control with a wholesome discretion, the remedy is not to take it from them, but to inform their discretion by education."

—Thomas Jefferson

CONTENTS

FOREWORD

On May 30, 1961, President Kennedy departed for Europe and a summit meeting with Khrushchev. Every day the Presidential tour was given banner headlines; and the meeting with Khrushchev was reported as an event of earth-shaking consequence.

It was an important event. But a meeting which was probably far more important, and which had commanded no front-page headlines at all, ended quietly on May 29, the day before President and Mrs. Kennedy set out on their grand tour.

On May 12, 1961, Dr. Philip E. Mosely, Director of Studies of the Council on Foreign Relations, announced that,

> "Prominent Soviet and American citizens will hold a week-long unofficial conference on Soviet-American relations in the Soviet Union, beginning May 22."

Dr. Mosely, a co-chairman of the American group, said that the State Department had approved the meeting but that the Americans involved would go as "private citizens" and would express their own views.

The New York Times' news story on Dr. Mosely's announcement (May 13, 1961) read:

> "The importance attached by the Soviet Union to the meeting appears to be suggested by the fact that the Soviet group will include three members of the communist party's Central Committee . . . and one candidate member of that body . . .

11

"The meeting, to be held in the town of Nizhnyaya Oreanda, in the Crimea, will follow the pattern of a similar unofficial meeting, in which many of the same persons participated, at Dartmouth College last fall. The meetings will take place in private and there are no plans to issue an agreed statement on the subjects discussed . . .

"The topics to be discussed include disarmament and the guaranteeing of . . . international peace, the role of the United Nations in strengthening international security, the role of advanced nations in aiding under-developed countries, and the prospects for peaceful and improving Soviet-United States relations.

"The Dartmouth conference last fall and the scheduled Crimean conference originated from a suggestion made by Norman Cousins, editor of The Saturday Review and co-chairman of the American group going to the Crimea, when he visited the Soviet Union a year and a half ago . . .

"Mr. Cousins and Dr. Mosely formed a small American group early last year to organize the conferences. It received financial support from the Ford Foundation for the Dartmouth conference and for travel costs to the Crimean meeting. This group selected the American representatives for the two meetings.

"Among those who participated in the Dartmouth conference were several who have since taken high posts in the Kennedy Administration, including Dr. Walt W. Rostow, now an assistant to President Kennedy, and George F. Kennan; now United States Ambassador to Yugoslavia . . ."

* * * * *

The head of the Soviet delegation to the meeting in the Soviet Union, May 22, 1961, was Alekesander Y. Korneichuk, a close personal friend of

Khrushchev. The American citizens scheduled to attend included besides Dr. Mosely and Mr. Cousins:

Marian Anderson, the singer; Dean Erwin N. Griswold, of the Harvard Law School; Gabriel Hauge, former economic adviser to President Eisenhower and now an executive of the Manufacturers Trust Company; Dr. Margaret Mead, a widely known anthropologist whose name (like that of Norman Cousins) has been associated with communist front activities in the United States; Dr. A. William Loos, Director of the Church Peace Union; Stuart Chase, American author notable for his pro-socialist, anti-anti-communist attitudes; William Benton, former U.S. Senator, also well-known as a pro-socialist, anti-anti-communist, now Chairman of the Board of Encyclopaedia Britannica; Dr. George Fisher, of the Massachusetts Institute of Technology; Professor Paul M. Doty, Jr., of Harvard's Chemistry Department; Professor Lloyd Reynolds, Yale University economist; Professor Louis B. Sohn of the Harvard Law School; Dr. Joseph E. Johnson, an old friend and former associate of Alger Hiss in the State Department, who succeeded Hiss as President of the Carnegie Endowment for International Peace, and still holds that position; Professor Robert R. Bowie, former head of the State Department's Policy Planning Staff (a job which Hiss also held at one time), now Director of the Center for International Affairs at Harvard; and Dr. Arthur Larson, former assistant to, and ghost writer for, President Eisenhower. Larson was often called "Mr. Modern Republican," because the political philosophy which he espoused was precisely that of Eisenhower (Larson is now, 1962, Director of the World Rule of Law Center at Duke University, where his full-time preoccupation is working for repeal of the Connally Reservation, so that the World Court can take jurisdiction over United States affairs).

* * * * *

I think the meeting which the Council on Foreign Relations arranged in the Soviet Union, in 1961, was more important than President Kennedy's meeting with Khrushchev, because I am convinced that the Council on Foreign Relations, together with a great number of other associated tax-exempt organizations, constitutes the invisible government which sets the major policies of the federal government; exercises controlling influence on governmental officials who implement the policies; and, through massive and skillful propaganda, influences Congress and the public to support the policies.

I am convinced that the objective of this invisible government is to convert America into a socialist state and then make it a unit in a one-world socialist system.

My convictions about the invisible government are based on information which is presented in this book.

The information about membership and activities of the Council on Foreign Relations and of its interlocking affiliates comes largely from publications issued by those organizations. I am deeply indebted to countless individuals who, when they learned of my interest, enriched my own files with material they had been collecting for years, hoping that someone would eventually use it.

I have not managed to get all of the membership rosters and publications issued by all of the organizations discussed. Hence, there are gaps in my information.

* * * * *

One aspect of the over-all subject, omitted entirely from this book, is the working relationship between internationalist groups in the United States and comparable groups abroad.

The Royal Institute of International Affairs in England (usually called Chatham House) and the American Council on Foreign Relations were both conceived at a dinner meeting in Paris in 1919. By working with the

CFR, the Royal Institute, undoubtedly, has had profound influence on American affairs.

Other internationalist organizations in foreign lands which work with the American Council on Foreign Relations, include the Institut des Relations Internationales (Belgium), Danish Foreign Policy Society, Indian Council of World Affairs, Australian Institute of International Affairs, and similar organizations in France, Italy, Yugoslavia, Greece, and Turkey.

The "Bilderbergers" are another powerful group involved in the internationalist web. The "Bilderbergers" take their name from the scene of their first known meeting—the Bilderberg Hotel, Oosterbeck, The Netherlands, in May, 1954. The group consists of influential Western businessmen, diplomats, and high governmental officials. Their meetings, conducted in secrecy and in a hugger-mugger atmosphere, are held about every six months at various places throughout the world. His Royal Highness, Prince Bernhard of The Netherlands, has presided at every known meeting of the Bilderberger Group.

Prince Bernhard is known to be an influential member of the Societé Generale de Belgique, a mysterious organization which seems to be an association of large corporate interests from many countries. American firms associated with the society are said to be among the large corporations whose officers are members of the Council on Foreign Relations and related organizations. I make no effort to explore this situation in this volume.

My confession of limitation upon my research does not embarrass me, because two committees of Congress have also failed to make a complete investigation of the great camarilla which manipulates our government. And the congressional committees were trying to investigate only one part of the web—the powerful tax-exempt foundations in the United States.

My own research does reveal the broad outlines of the invisible government.

D.S.
May, 1962

CHAPTER 1.

HISTORY AND THE COUNCIL

President George Washington, in his Farewell Address to the People of the United States on September 17, 1796, established a foreign policy which became traditional and a main article of faith for the American people in their dealings with the rest of the world.

Washington warned against foreign influence in the shaping of national affairs. He urged America to avoid permanent, entangling alliances with other nations, recommending a national policy of benign neutrality toward the rest of the world. Washington did not want America to build a wall around herself, or to become, in any sense, a hermit nation. Washington's policy permitted freer exchange of travel, commerce, ideas, and culture between Americans and other people than Americans have ever enjoyed since the policy was abandoned. The Father of our Country wanted the American government to be kept out of the wars and revolutions and political affairs of other nations.

Washington told Americans that their nation had a high destiny, which it could not fulfill if they permitted their government to become entangled in the affairs of other nations.

Despite the fact of two foreign wars (Mexican War, 1846-1848; and Spanish American War, 1898) the foreign policy of Washington remained the policy of this nation, unaltered, for 121 years—until Woodrow Wilson's war message to Congress in April, 1917.

* * * * *

Wilson himself, when campaigning for re-election in 1916, had unequivocally supported our traditional foreign policy: his one major promise to the American people was that he would keep them out of the European war.

Yet, even while making this promise, Wilson was yielding to a pressure he was never able to withstand: the influence of Colonel Edward M. House, Wilson's all-powerful adviser. According to House's own papers and the historical studies of Wilson's ardent admirers (see, for example, Intimate Papers of Colonel House, edited by Charles Seymour, published in 1926 by Houghton Mifflin; and, The Crisis of the Old Order by Arthur M. Schlesinger, Jr., published 1957 by Houghton Mifflin), House created Wilson's domestic and foreign policies, selected most of Wilson's cabinet and other major appointees, and ran Wilson's State Department.

House had powerful connections with international bankers in New York. He was influential, for example, with great financial institutions represented by such people as Paul and Felix Warburg, Otto H. Kahn, Louis Marburg, Henry Morgenthau, Jacob and Mortimer Schiff, Herbert Lehman. House had equally powerful connections with bankers and politicians of Europe.

Bringing all of these forces to bear, House persuaded Wilson that America had an evangelistic mission to save the world for "democracy." The first major twentieth century tragedy for the United States resulted: Wilson's war message to Congress and the declaration of war against Germany on April 6, 1917.

House also persuaded Wilson that the way to avoid all future wars was to create a world federation of nations. On May 27, 1916, in a speech to the League to Enforce Peace, Wilson first publicly endorsed Colonel House's world-government idea (without, however, identifying it as originating with House).

In September, 1916, Wilson (at the urging of House) appointed a committee of intellectuals (the first President's Brain Trust) to formulate peace terms and draw up a charter for world government. This committee, with House in charge, consisted of about 150 college professors, graduate students, lawyers, economists, writers, and others. Among them were men still familiar to Americans in the 1960's: Walter Lippmann (columnist); Norman Thomas (head of the American socialist party); Allen Dulles (former head of C.I.A.); John Foster Dulles (late Secretary of State); Christian A. Herter (former Secretary of State).

These eager young intellectuals around Wilson, under the clear eyes of crafty Colonel House, drew up their charter for world government (League of Nations Covenant) and prepared for the brave new socialist one-world to follow World War I. But things went sour at the Paris Peace Conference. They soured even more when constitutionalists in the United States Senate found out what was being planned and made it quite plain that the Senate would not authorize United States membership in such a world federation.

Bitter with disappointment but not willing to give up, Colonel House called together in Paris, France, a group of his most dedicated young intellectuals–among them, John Foster and Allen Dulles, Christian A. Herter, and Tasker H. Bliss–and arranged a dinner meeting with a group of like-minded Englishmen at the Majestic Hotel, Paris, on May 19, 1919. The group formally agreed to form an organization "for the study of international affairs."

The American group came home from Paris and formed The Council on Foreign Relations, which was incorporated in 1921.

The purpose of the Council on Foreign Relations was to create (and condition the American people to accept) what House called a "positive" foreign policy for America–to replace the traditional "negative" foreign policy which had kept America out of the endless turmoil of old-world politics and had permitted the American people to develop their great nation in freedom and independence from the rest of the world.

The Council did not amount to a great deal until 1927, when the Rockefeller family (through the various Rockefeller Foundations and Funds) began to pour money into it. Before long, the Carnegie Foundations (and later the Ford Foundation) began to finance the Council.

In 1929, the Council (largely with Rockefeller gifts) acquired its present headquarters property: The Harold Pratt House, 58 East 68th Street, New York City.

In 1939, the Council began taking over the U.S. State Department.

Shortly after the start of World War II, in September, 1939, Hamilton Fish Armstrong and Walter H. Mallory, of the Council on Foreign Relations, visited the State Department to offer the services of the Council. It was agreed that the Council would do research and make recommendations for the State Department, without formal assignment or responsibility. The Council formed groups to work in four general fields–Security and Armaments Problems, Economic and Financial Problems, Political Problems, and Territorial Problems.

The Rockefeller Foundation agreed to finance, through grants, the operation of this plan.

In February, 1941, the Council on Foreign Relations' relationship with the State Department changed. The State Department created the Division of Special Research, which was divided into Economic, Security, Political, Territorial sections. Leo Pasvolsky, of the Council, was appointed Director of this Division. Within a very short time, members of the Council on Foreign Relations dominated this new Division in the State Department.

During 1942, the State Department set up the Advisory Committee on Postwar Foreign Policy. Secretary of State Cordell Hull was Chairman. The following members of the Council on Foreign Relations were on this Committee: Under Secretary of State Sumner Welles (Vice-Chairman), Dr. Leo Pasvolsky (Executive Officer); Hamilton Fish Armstrong,

Isaiah Bowman, Benjamin V. Cohen, Norman H. Davis, and James T. Shotwell.

Other members of the Council also found positions in the State Department: Philip E. Mosely, Walter E. Sharp, and Grayson Kirk, among others.

The crowning moment of achievement for the Council came at San Francisco in 1945, when over 40 members of the United States Delegation to the organizational meeting of the United Nations (where the United Nations Charter was written) were members of the Council. Among them: Alger Hiss, Secretary of State Edward R. Stettinius, Leo Pasvolsky, John Foster Dulles, John J. McCloy, Julius C. Holmes, Nelson A. Rockefeller, Adlai Stevenson, Joseph E. Johnson, Ralph J. Bunche, Clark M. Eichelberger, and Thomas K. Finletter.

By 1945, the Council on Foreign Relations, and various foundations and other organizations interlocked with it, had virtually taken over the U.S. State Department.

Some CFR members were later identified as Soviet espionage agents: for example, Alger Hiss and Lauchlin Currie.

Other Council on Foreign Relations members—Owen Lattimore, for example—with powerful influence in the Roosevelt and Truman Administrations, were subsequently identified, not as actual communists or Soviet espionage agents, but as "conscious, articulate instruments of the Soviet international conspiracy."

I do not intend to imply by these citations that the Council on Foreign Relations is, or ever was, a communist organization. Boasting among its members Presidents of the United States (Hoover, Eisenhower, and Kennedy), Secretaries of State, and many other high officials, both civilian and military, the Council can be termed, by those who agree with its objectives, a "patriotic" organization.

The fact, however, that communists, Soviet espionage agents, and pro-communists could work inconspicuously for many years as influential members of the Council indicates something very significant about the

Council's objectives. The ultimate aim of the Council on Foreign Relations (however well-intentioned its prominent and powerful members may be) is the same as the ultimate aim of international communism: to create a one-world socialist system and make the United States an official part of it.

Some indication of the influence of CFR members can be found in the boasts of their best friends. Consider the remarkable case of the nomination and confirmation of Julius C. Holmes as United States Ambassador to Iran. Holmes was one of the CFR members who served as United States delegates to the United Nations founding conference at San Francisco in 1945.

Mr. Holmes has had many important jobs in the State Department since 1925; but from 1945 to 1948, he was out of government service.

During that early postwar period, the United States government had approximately 390 Merchant Marine oil tankers (built and used during World War II) which had become surplus.

A law of Congress prohibited the government from selling the surplus vessels to foreign-owned or foreign-controlled companies, and prohibited any American company from purchasing them for resale to foreigners.

The purpose of the law was to guarantee that oil tankers (vital in times of war) would remain under the control of the United States government.

Julius Holmes conceived the idea of making a quick profit by buying and selling some of the surplus tankers.

Holmes was closely associated with Edward Stettinius, former Secretary of State, and with two of Stettinius' principal advisers: Joe Casey, a former U.S. Congressman; and Stanley Klein, a New York financier.

In August, 1947, this group formed a corporation (and ultimately formed others) to buy surplus oil tankers from the government. The legal and technical maneuvering which followed is complex and shady, but it has all been revealed and reported by congressional committees.

Holmes and his associates managed to buy eight oil tankers from the U.S. government and re-sell all of them to foreign interests, in violation of the intent of the law and of the surplus-disposal program. One of the eight tankers was ultimately leased to the Soviet Union and used to haul fuel oil from communist Romania to the Chinese reds during the Korean war.

By the time he returned to foreign service with the State Department in September, 1948, Holmes had made for himself an estimated profit of about one million dollars, with practically no investment of his own money, and at no financial risk.

A Senate subcommittee, which, in 1952, investigated this affair, unanimously condemned the Holmes-Casey-Klein tanker deals as "morally wrong and clearly in violation of the intent of the law," and as a "highly improper, if not actually illegal, get-rich-quick" operation which was detrimental to the interests of the United States.

Holmes and his associates were criminally indicted in 1954–but the Department of Justice dismissed the indictments on a legal technicality later that same year.

A few weeks after the criminal indictment against Holmes had been dismissed, President Eisenhower, in 1955, nominated Julius C. Holmes to be our Ambassador to Iran.

Enough United States Senators in 1955 expressed a decent sense of outrage about the nomination of such a man for such a post that Holmes "permitted" his name to be withdrawn, before the Senate acted on the question of confirming his appointment.

The State Department promptly sent Holmes to Tangier with the rank of Minister; brought him back to Washington in 1956 as a Special Assistant to the Secretary of State; and sent him out as Minister and Consul General in Hong Kong and Macao in 1959.

And then, in 1961, Kennedy nominated Julius C. Holmes for the same job Eisenhower had tried to give him in 1955–Ambassador to Iran.

Arguing in favor of Holmes, Senator Prescott Bush admitted that Holmes' tanker deals were improper and ill-advised, but claimed that Holmes was an innocent victim of sharp operators! The "innocent" victim made a million dollars in one year by being victimized. He has never offered to make restitution to the government. Moreover, when questioned, in April, 1961, Holmes said he still sees nothing wrong with what he did and admits he would do it again if he had the opportunity—and felt that no congressional committee would ever investigate.

All Senators, who supported Holmes in debate, hammered the point that, although Holmes may have done something shady and unsavory during the three-year period in the late 1940's when he was out of government service, there was no evidence that he had ever misbehaved while he was in government service.

This amoral attitude seems to imply that a known chicken thief cannot be considered a threat to turkey growers, unless he has actually been caught stealing turkeys.

Senate debates on the confirmation of Holmes as Ambassador to Iran are printed in the Congressional Record: pp. 6385-86, April 27, 1961; pp. 6668-69, May 3, 1961; and pp. 6982-95, May 8, 1961.

The vote was taken on May 8. After the history of Julius C. Holmes had been thoroughly exposed, the Senate confirmed Holmes' nomination 75 to 21, with 4 Senators taking no stand. Julius C. Holmes was sworn in as United States Ambassador to Iran on May 15, 1961.

The real reason why Holmes was nominated for an important ambassadorship by two Presidents and finally confirmed by the Senate is obvious—and was, indeed, inadvertently revealed by Senator Prescott Bush: Holmes, a Council on Foreign Relations member, is a darling of the leftwing internationalists who are determined to drag America into a socialist one-world system.

During the Senate debate about Holmes' nomination Senator Bush said:

"I believe that one of the most telling witnesses with whom I have ever talked regarding Mr. Holmes is Mr. Henry Wriston, formerly president of Brown University, now chairman of the Council on Foreign Relations, in New York, and chairman of the American Assembly. Mr. Wriston not only holds these distinguished offices, but he has also made a special study of the State Department and the career service in the State Department.

"He is credited with having 'Wristonized' the Foreign Service of the United States. He told me a few years ago . . . [that] 'Julius Holmes is the ablest man in the Foreign Service Corps of the United States.'"

Dr. Wriston was (in 1961) President (not Chairman, as Senator Bush called him) of the Council on Foreign Relations. But Senator Bush was not exaggerating or erring when he said that the State Department has been Wristonized–if we acknowledge that the State Department has been converted into an agency of Dr. Wriston's Council on Foreign Relations. Indeed, the Senator could have said that the United States government has been Wristonized.

Here, for example, are some of the members of the Council on Foreign Relations who, in 1961, held positions in the United States Government: John F. Kennedy, President; Dean Rusk, Secretary of State; Douglas Dillon, Secretary of the Treasury; Adlai Stevenson, United Nations Ambassador; Allen W. Dulles, Director of the Central Intelligence Agency; Chester Bowles, Under Secretary of State; W. Averell Harriman, Ambassador-at-large; John J. McCloy, Disarmament Administrator; General Lyman L. Lemnitzer, Chairman of the Joint Chiefs of Staff; John Kenneth Galbraith, Ambassador to India; Edward R. Murrow, Head of United States Information Agency; G. Frederick Reinhardt, Ambassador to Italy; David K. E. Bruce, Ambassador to United Kingdom; Livingston T. Merchant, Ambassador to Canada; Lt. Gen. James M. Gavin, Ambassador to France; George F. Kennan, Ambassador to

Yugoslavia; Julius C. Holmes, Ambassador to Iran; Arthur H. Dean, head of the United States Delegation to Geneva Disarmament Conference; Arthur M. Schlesinger, Jr., Special White House Assistant; Edwin O. Reischauer, Ambassador to Japan; Thomas K. Finletter, Ambassador to the North Atlantic Treaty Organization for Economic Co-operation and Development; George C. McGhee, Assistant Secretary of State for Policy Planning; Henry R. Labouisse, Director of International Cooperation Administration; George W. Ball, Under Secretary of State for Economic Affairs; McGeorge Bundy, Special Assistant for National Security; Paul H. Nitze, Assistant Secretary of Defense; Adolf A. Berle, Chairman, Inter-Departmental Committee on Latin America; Charles E. Bohlen, Assistant Secretary of State.

The names listed do not, by any means, constitute a complete roster of all Council members who are in the Congress or hold important positions in the Administration.

In the 1960-61 Annual Report of the Council on Foreign Relations, there is an item of information which reveals a great deal about the close relationship between the Council and the executive branch of the federal government.

On Page 37, The Report explains why there had been an unusually large recent increase in the number of non-resident members (CFR members who do not reside within 50 miles of New York City Hall):

"The rather large increase in the non-resident academic category is largely explained by the fact that many academic members have left New York to join the new administration."

* * * * *

Concerning President Kennedy's membership in the CFR, there is an interesting story. On June 7, 1960, Mr. Kennedy, then a United States

Senator, wrote a letter answering a question about his membership in the Council. Mr. Kennedy said:

"I am a member of the Council on Foreign Relations in New York City. As a long-time subscriber to the quarterly, Foreign Affairs, and as a member of the Senate, I was invited to become a member."

On August 23, 1961, Mr. George S. Franklin, Jr., Executive Director of the Council on Foreign Relations, wrote a letter answering a question about President Kennedy's membership. Mr. Franklin said:

"I am enclosing the latest Annual Report of the Council with a list of members in the back. You will note that President Eisenhower is a member, but this is not true of either President Kennedy or President Truman."

President Kennedy is not listed as a member in the 1960-61 Annual Report of the CFR.

The complete roster of CFR members, as set out in the 1960-61 Annual Report, is in Appendix I of this volume. Several persons, besides President Kennedy, whom I have called CFR members are not on this roster. I have called them CFR members, if their names have ever appeared on any official CFR membership list.

The Council is actually a small organization. Its membership is restricted to 700 resident members (American citizens whose residences or places of business are within 50 miles of City Hall in New York City), and 700 non-resident members (American citizens who reside or do business outside that 50-mile radius); but most of the members occupy important positions in government, in education, in the press, in the broadcasting industry, in business, in finance, or in some multi-million-dollar tax-exempt foundation.

An indication of overall accomplishments of the Council can be found in its Annual Report of 1958-59, which reprints a speech by Walter H. Mallory on the occasion of his retiring after 32 years as Executive Director of the Council. Speaking to the Board of Directors of the Council at a small dinner in his honor on May 21, 1959, Mr. Mallory said:

> "When I cast my mind back to 1927, the year that I first joined the Council, it seems little short of a miracle that the organization could have taken root in those days. You will remember that the United States had decided not to join the League of Nations . . . On the domestic front, the budget was extremely small, taxes were light . . . and we didn't even recognize the Russians. What could there possibly be for a Council on Foreign Relations to do?
>
> "Well, there were a few men who did not feel content with that comfortable isolationist climate. They thought the United States had an important role to play in the world and they resolved to try to find out what that role ought to be. Some of those men are present this evening."

The Council's principal publication is a quarterly magazine, Foreign Affairs. Indeed, publishing this quarterly is the Council's major activity; and income from the publication is a principal source of revenue for the Council.

On June 30, 1961, Foreign Affairs had a circulation of only 43,500; but it is probably the most influential publication in the world. Key figures in government—from the Secretary of State downward—write articles for, and announce new policies in, Foreign Affairs.

Other publications of the Council include three volumes which it publishes annually (Political Handbook of the World, The United States in World Affairs and Documents on American Foreign Relations), and numerous special studies and books.

The Council's financial statement for the 1960-61 fiscal year listed the following income:

Membership Dues	$123,200
Council Development Fund	$ 87,000
Committees Development Fund	$ 2,500
Corporation Service	$112,200
Foundation Grants	$231,700
Net Income from Investments	$106,700
Net Receipt from Sale of Books	$ 26,700
Foreign Affairs Subscriptions and Sales	$210,300
Foreign Affairs Advertising	$ 21,800
Miscellaneous	$ 2,900
	—————
Total	$925,000

"Corporation Service" on this list means money contributed to the Council by business firms.

Here are firms listed as contributors to the Council during the 1960-61 fiscal year:

Aluminum Limited, Inc.
American Can Company
American Metal Climax, Inc.
American Telephone and Telegraph Company
Arabian American Oil Company
Armco International Corporation
Asiatic Petroleum Corporation
Bankers Trust Company
Belgian Securities Corporation
Bethlehem Steel Company, Inc.
Brown Brothers, Harriman and Co.
Cabot Corporation
California Texas Oil Corp.

Cameron Iron Works, Inc.
Campbell Soup Company
The Chase Manhattan Bank
Chesebrough-Pond's Inc.
Chicago Bridge and Iron Co.
Cities Service Company, Inc.
Connecticut General Life Insurance Company
Continental Can Company
Continental Oil Company
Corn Products Company
Corning Glass Works
Dresser Industries, Inc.
Ethyl Corporation
I. I. du Pont de Nemours & Co., Inc.
Farrell Lines, Inc.
The First National City Bank of New York
Ford Motor Company, International Division
Foster Wheeler Corporation
Freeport Sulphur Company
General Dynamics Corporation
General Motors Overseas Operations
The Gillette Company
W. R. Grace and Co.
Gulf Oil Corporation
Halliburton Oil Well Cementing Company
Haskins and Sells
H. J. Heinz Company
Hughes Tool Company
IBM World Trade Corporation
International General Electric Company
The International Nickel Company, Inc.
International Telephone and Telegraph Corporation

Irving Trust Company
The M. W. Kellogg Company
Kidder, Peabody and Co.
Carl M. Loeb, Rhoades and Co.
The Lummus Company
Merck and Company, Inc.
Mobil International Oil Co.
Model, Roland and Stone
The National Cash Register Co.
National Lead Company, Inc.
The New York Times
The Ohio Oil Co., Inc.
Olin Mathieson Chemical Corporation
Otis Elevator Company
Owens-Corning Fiberglas Corporation
Pan American Airways System
Pfizer International, Inc.
Radio Corporation of America
The RAND Corporation
San Jacinto Petroleum Corporation
J. Henry Schroder Banking Corporation
Sinclair Oil Corporation
The Singer Manufacturing Company
Sprague Electric Company
Standard Oil Company of California
Standard Oil Company (N. J.)
Standard-Vacuum Oil Company
Stauffer Chemical Company
Symington Wayne Corporation
Texaco, Inc.
Texas Gulf Sulphur Company
Texas Instruments, Inc.

Tidewater Oil Company
Time, Inc.
Union Tank Car Company
United States Lines Company
United States Steel Corporation
White, Weld and Co.
Wyandotte Chemicals Corporation

What do these corporations get for the money contributed to the Council on Foreign Relations?

From the 1960-61 Annual Report of the Council:

"Subscribers to the Council's Corporation Service (who pay a minimum fee of $1,000) are entitled to several privileges. Among them are (a) free consultation with members of the Council's staff on problems of foreign policy, (b) access to the Council's specialized library on international affairs, including its unique collection of magazine and press clippings, (c) copies of all Council publications and six subscriptions to Foreign Affairs for officers of the company or its library, (d) an off-the-record dinner, held annually for chairmen and presidents of subscribing companies at which a prominent speaker discusses some outstanding issue of United States foreign policy, and (e) two annual series of Seminars for business executives appointed by their companies. These Seminars are led by widely experienced Americans who discuss various problems of American political or economic foreign policy."

All speakers at the Council's dinner meetings and seminars for business executives are leading advocates of internationalism and the total state. Many of them, in fact, are important officials in government. The ego-appeal is enormous to businessmen, who get special off-the-record briefings from Cabinet officers and other officials close to the President of the United States.

The briefings and the seminar lectures are consistently designed to elicit the support of businessmen for major features of Administration policy.

For example, during 1960 and 1961, the three issues of major importance to both Presidents Eisenhower and Kennedy were Disarmament, the declining value of the American dollar, and the tariff-and-trade problem. The Eisenhower and Kennedy positions on these three issues were virtually identical; and the solutions they urged meshed with the internationalist program of pushing America into a one-world socialist system.

The business executives who attended CFR briefings and seminars in the 1960-61 fiscal year received expert indoctrination in the internationalist position on the three major issues of that year. From "Seminars For Business Executives," Pages 43-44 of the 1960-61 Annual Report of the Council on Foreign Relations:

"The Fall 1960 Seminar . . . was brought to a close with an appraisal of disarmament negotiations, past and present, by Edmund A. Gullion, then Acting Deputy Director, United States Disarmament Administration . . .

"'The International Position of the Dollar' was the theme of the Spring 1961 Seminar series. Robert Triffin, Professor of Economics at Yale University, spoke on the present balance of payments situation at the opening session. At the second meeting, William Diebold, Jr., Director of Economic Studies at the Council, addressed the group on United States foreign trade policy. The third meeting dealt with foreign investment and the balance of payments. August Maffry, Vice President of the Irving Trust Company, was discussion leader . . .

"On June 8, George W. Ball, Under Secretary of State for Economic Affairs, spoke at the annual Corporation Service dinner for presidents and board chairmen of participating companies . . . Secretary Ball [discussed] the foreign economic policy of the new Kennedy Administration."

George W. Ball was, for several years, a registered lobbyist in Washington, representing foreign commercial interests. He is a chief architect of President Kennedy's 1962 tariff-and-trade proposals—which would internationalize American trade and commerce, as a prelude to amalgamating our economy with that of other nations.

In 1960-61, 84 leading corporations contributed 112,200 tax-exempt dollars to the Council on Foreign Relations for the privilege of having their chief officers exposed to the propaganda of international socialism.

A principal activity of the Council is its meetings, according to the 1958-1959 annual report:

"During 1958-59, the Council's program of meetings continued to place emphasis on small, roundtable meetings . . . Of the 99 meetings held during the year, 58 were roundtables . . . The balance of the meetings program was made up of the more traditional large afternoon or dinner sessions for larger groups of Council members. In the course of the year, the Council convened such meetings for Premier Castro; First Deputy Premier Mikoyan; Secretary-General Dag Hammarskjold . . ."

The Council's annual report lists all of the meetings and "distinguished" speakers for which it convened the meetings. It is an amazing list. Although the Council has tax-exemption as an organization to study international affairs and, presumably, to help the public arrive at a better understanding of United States foreign policy, not one speaker for any Council meeting represented traditional U. S. policy. Every one was a known advocate of leftwing internationalism. A surprising number of them were known communists or communist sympathizers or admitted socialists.

34

Kwame Nkrumah, Prime Minister of Ghana, who is widely believed to be a communist; who is admittedly socialist; and who aligned his nation with the Soviets–spoke to the Council on "Free Africa," with W. Averell Harriman presiding.

Mahmoud Fawzi, Minister of Foreign Affairs of the United Arab Republic, a socialist whose hatred of the United States is rather well known, spoke to the Council on "Middle East."

Herbert L. Matthews, a member of the editorial board of The New York Times (whose articles on Castro as the Robin Hood of Cuba built that communist hoodlum a worldwide reputation and helped him conquer Cuba) spoke to the Council twice, once on "A Political Appraisal of Latin American Affairs," and once on "The Castro Regime."

M. C. Chagla, Ambassador of India to the United States, a socialist, spoke to the Council on "Indian Foreign Policy."

Anastas I. Mikoyan, First Deputy Premier, USSR, spoke to the Council on "Issues in Soviet-American Relations," with John J. McCloy (later Kennedy's Disarmament Administrator) presiding.

Fidel Castro spoke to the Council on "Cuba and the United States."

Here are some other well-known socialists who spoke to the Council on Foreign Relations during the 1958-59 year:

Dag Hammarskjold, Secretary-General of the United Nations; Per Jacobsson, Managing Director of the International Monetary Fund; Abba Eban, Ambassador of Israel to the United States; Willy Brandt, Mayor of West Berlin; Stanley de Zoysa, Minister of Finance of Ceylon; Mortarji Desai, Minister of Finance of India; Victor Urquidi, President of Mexican Economic Society; Fritz Erler, Co-Chairman of the Socialist Group in the German Bundestag; Tom Mboya, Member of the Kenya Legislative Council; Sir Grantley H. Adams, Prime Minister of the West Indies Federation; Theodore Kollek, Director-General of the Office of the Prime Minister of Israel; Dr. Gikomyo W. Kiano, member of the Kenya Legislative Council.

Officials of communist governments, in addition to those already listed, who spoke to the Council that year, included Oscar Lange, Vice-President of the State Council of the Polish People's Republic; and Marko Nikezic, Ambassador of Yugoslavia to the United States.

* * * * *

Throughout this book, I show the close inter-locking connection between the Council on Foreign Relations and many other organizations. The only organizations formally affiliated with the Council, however, are the Committees on Foreign Relations, which the Council created, which it controls, and which exist in 30 cities: Albuquerque, Atlanta, Birmingham, Boise, Boston, Casper, Charlottesville, Denver, Des Moines, Detroit, Houston, Indianapolis, Little Rock, Los Angeles, Louisville, Nashville, Omaha, Philadelphia, Portland (Maine), Portland (Oregon), Providence, St. Louis, St. Paul-Minneapolis, Salt Lake City, San Francisco, Seattle, Tucson, Tulsa, Wichita, Worcester.

A booklet entitled Committees on Foreign Relations: Directory of Members, January, 1961, published by the Council on Foreign Relations, contains a roster of members of all the Committees on Foreign Relations, except the one at Casper, Wyoming, which was not organized until later in 1961. The booklet also gives a brief history of the Committees:

> "In 1938, with the financial assistance of the Carnegie Corporation of New York, the Council began to organize affiliated discussion groups in a few American cities . . .
>
> "Each Committee is composed of forty or more men who are leaders in the professions and occupations of their area—representatives of business, the law, universities and schools, the press, and so on. About once a month, from October through May, members come together for dinner and an evening of discussion with a guest speaker of special competence . . . Since the beginning

in 1938, the Carnegie Corporation of New York has continued to make annual grants in support of the Committee program."

The following information about the Committees on Foreign Relations is from the 1960-61 Annual Report of the Council on Foreign Relations:

"During the past season the Foreign Relations Committees carried on their customary programs of private dinner meetings. In all, 206 meetings were held . . .

"The Council arranged or figured in the arrangement of about three-quarters of the meetings held, the other sessions being undertaken upon the initiative of the Committees. Attendance at the discussions averaged 28 persons, slightly more than in previous years and about the maximum number for good discussion. There was little change in membership–the total being just under 1800. It will be recalled that this membership consists of men who are leaders in the various professions and occupations . . .

"On June 2 and 3, the 23rd annual conference of Committee representatives was held at the Harold Pratt House. Mounting pressures throughout the year . . . made it advisable to plan a conference program that would facilitate re-examination of the strategic uses of the United Nations for American Policy in the years ahead. Accordingly, the conference theme was designated as United States Policy and the United Nations. Emphasis was upon re-appraisal of the United States national interest in the United Nations–and the cost of sustaining that interest . . .

"In the course of the year, officers and members of the Council and of the staff visited most of the Committees for the purpose of leading discussions at meetings, supervising Committee procedures and seeking the strengthening of Committee relations with the Council."

CHAPTER 2.

WORLD WAR II AND
TRAGIC CONSEQUENCES

Although the Council on Foreign Relations had almost gained controlling influence on the government of the United States as early as 1941, it had failed to indoctrinate the American people for acceptance of what Colonel House had called a "positive" foreign policy.

In 1940, Franklin D. Roosevelt (although eager to get the United States into the Second World War and already making preparations for that tragedy) had to campaign for re-election with the same promise that Wilson had made in 1916–to keep us out of the European war. Even as late as the day before the Japanese attack on Pearl Harbor in December, 1941, the American people were still overwhelmingly "isolationist"–a word which internationalists use as a term of contempt but which means merely that the American people were still devoted to their nation's traditional foreign policy.

It was necessary for Roosevelt to take steps which the public would not notice or understand but which would inescapably involve the nation in the foreign war. When enough such sly involvement had been manipulated, there would come, eventually, some incident to push us over the brink into open participation. Then, any American who continued to advocate our traditional foreign policy of benign neutrality would be an object of public hatred, would be investigated and condemned by officialdom as a "pro-nazi," and possibly prosecuted for sedition.

The Council on Foreign Relations has heavy responsibility for the maneuvering which thus dragged America into World War II. One major step which Roosevelt took toward war (at precisely the time when he was campaigning for his third-term re-election on a platform of peace and neutrality to keep America out of war) was his radical alteration of traditional concepts of United States policy in order to declare Greenland under the protection of our Monroe Doctrine. The Council on Foreign Relations officially boasts full responsibility for this fateful step toward war.

On pages 13 and 14 of a book entitled The Council on Foreign Relations: A Record of Twenty-Five Years, 1921-1946 (written by officials of the Council and published by the Council on January 1, 1947) are these passages:

"One further example may be cited of the way in which ideas and recommendations originating at Council meetings have entered into the stream of official discussion and action.

"On March 17, 1940, a Council group completed a confidential report which pointed out the strategic importance of Greenland for transatlantic aviation and for meteorological observations. The report stated:

"'The possibility must be considered that Denmark might be overrun by Germany. In such case, Greenland might be transferred by treaty to German sovereignty.'

"It also pointed out the possible danger to the United States in such an eventuality, and mentioned that Greenland lies within the geographical sphere 'within which the Monroe Doctrine is presumed to apply.'

"Shortly after this, one of the members of the group which had prepared the report was summoned to the White House.

President Roosevelt had a copy of the memorandum in his hand and said that he had turned to his visitor for advice because of his part in raising the question of Greenland's strategic importance.

"Germany invaded Denmark on April 9, 1940. At his press conference three days later, the President stated that he was satisfied that Greenland was a part of the American continent. After a visit to the White House on the same day, the Danish Minister said that he agreed with the President.

"On April 9, 1941, an agreement was signed between the United States and Denmark which provided for assistance by the United States to Greenland in the maintenance of its status, and granted to the United States the right to locate and construct such airplane landing-fields, seaplane facilities, and radio and meteorological installations as might be necessary for the defense of Greenland, and for the defense of the American continent. This was eight months before Germany declared war on the United States.

"The Council's report on Greenland was only one item in an extensive research project which offered an unusual instance of wartime collaboration between Government agencies and a private institution ... The project ... exhibited the kind of contribution which the Council has been uniquely equipped to provide ..."

* * * * *

The Danish colony of Greenland—a huge island covered by polar ice—lies in the Arctic Ocean, 1325 miles off the coast of Denmark. It is 200 miles from Canada, 650 miles from the British Isles. The extreme southwestern tip of Greenland is 1315 miles from the most extreme northeastern tip of the United States (Maine). In other words, Canada and England, which were at war with Germany when we undertook to protect Greenland from Germany, are both much closer to Greenland than the United States is.

40

But history gives better proof than geography does, that the learned Council members who put Greenland in the Western Hemisphere, within the meaning of the Monroe Doctrine, were either ignorant or dishonest. The Monroe Doctrine, closing the Western Hemisphere to further European colonization, was proclaimed in 1823. Denmark, a European nation, colonized Greenland, proclaiming sole sovereignty in 1921, without any hint of protest from the United States that this European colonization infringed upon the Monroe Doctrine.

* * * * *

Members of the Council on Foreign Relations played a key role in getting America into World War II. They played the role in creating the basic policies which this nation has followed since the end of World War II. These policies are accomplishing:

(1) the redistribution to other nations of the great United States reserve of gold which made our dollar the strongest currency in the world;

(2) the building up of the industrial capacity of other nations, at our expense, thus eliminating our pre-eminent productive superiority;

(3) the taking away of world markets from United States producers (and even much of their domestic market) until capitalistic America will no longer dominate world trade;

(4) the entwining of American affairs—economic, political, cultural, social, educational, and even religious—with those of other nations until the United States will no longer have an independent policy, either domestic or foreign: until we can not return to our traditional foreign policy of maintaining national independence, nor to free private capitalism as an economic system.

The ghastly wartime and post-war decisions (which put the Soviet Union astride the globe like a menacing colossus and placed the incomparably stronger United States in the position of appeasing and retreating) can be traced to persons who were members of the Council on Foreign Relations.

Consider a specific example: the explosive German problem.

* * * * *

In October, 1943, Cordell Hull (U. S. Secretary of State), Anthony Eden (Foreign Minister for Great Britain), and V. Molotov (Soviet Commissar for Foreign Affairs), had a conference at Moscow. Eden suggested that they create a European Advisory Commission which would decide how Germany, after defeat, would be partitioned, occupied, and governed by the three victorious powers. Molotov approved. Hull did not like the idea, but agreed to it in deference to the wishes of the two others. Philip E. Mosely, of the CFR, was Hull's special adviser at this Moscow Conference.

The next month, November, 1943, President Franklin D. Roosevelt went to Tehran for his first conference with Stalin and Churchill. Aboard the U. S. S. Iowa en route to Tehran, Roosevelt had a conference with his Joint Chiefs of Staff. They discussed, among other things, the post-war division and occupation of Germany.

President Roosevelt predicted that Germany would collapse suddenly and that "there would definitely be a race for Berlin" by the three great powers. The President said: "We may have to put the United States divisions into Berlin as soon as possible, because the United States should have Berlin."

Harry Hopkins suggested that "we be ready to put an airborne division into Berlin two hours after the collapse of Germany."

Roosevelt wanted the United States to occupy Berlin and northwestern Germany; the British to occupy France, Belgium, and southern Germany; and the Soviets to have eastern Germany.

At the Tehran Conference (November 27-December 2, 1943), Stalin seemed singularly indifferent to the question of which power would occupy which zones of Germany after the war. Stalin revealed intense interest in only three topics:

(1) urging the western allies to make a frontal assault, across the English Channel, on Hitler's fortress Europe;

(2) finding out, immediately, the name of the man whom the western allies would designate to command such an operation (Eisenhower had not yet been selected); and

(3) reducing the whole of Europe to virtual impotence so that the Soviet Union would be the only major power on the continent after the war.

Roosevelt approved of every proposal Stalin made.

A broad outline of the behavior and proposals of Roosevelt, Churchill, and Stalin at Tehran can be found in the diplomatic papers published in 1961 by the State Department, in a volume entitled Foreign Relations of the United States: Diplomatic Papers: The Conferences at Cairo and Tehran 1943.

As to specific agreements on the postwar division and occupation of Germany, the Tehran papers reveal only that the European Advisory Commission would work out the details.

We know that Roosevelt and his military advisers in November, 1943, agreed that America should take and occupy Berlin. Yet, 17 months later, we did just the opposite.

* * * * *

In the closing days of World War II, the American Ninth Army was rolling toward Berlin, meeting little resistance, slowed down only by German civilians clogging the highways, fleeing from the Russians. German soundtrucks were circulating in the Berlin area, counseling stray troops to stop resistance and surrender to the Americans. Some twenty or thirty miles east of Berlin, the German nation had concentrated its dying strength and was fighting savagely against the Russians.

Our Ninth Army could have been in Berlin within a few hours, probably without shedding another drop of blood; but General Eisenhower suddenly halted our Army. He kept it sitting idly outside Berlin for days, while the Russians slugged their way in, killing, raping, ravaging. We gave the Russians control of the eastern portion of Berlin—and of all the territory surrounding the city.

To the south, General Patton's forces were plowing into Czechoslovakia. When Patton was thirty miles from Prague, the capital, General Eisenhower ordered him to stop—ordered him not to accept surrender of German soldiers, but to hold them at bay until the Russians could move up and accept surrender. As soon as the Russians were thus established as the conquerors of Czechoslovakia, Eisenhower ordered Patton to evacuate.

Units of Czechoslovakian patriots had been fighting with Western armies since 1943. We had promised them that they could participate in the liberation of their own homeland; but we did not let them move into Czechoslovakia until after the Russians had taken over.

Czechoslovakian and American troops had to ask the Soviets for permission to come into Prague for a victory celebration—after the Russians had been permitted to conquer the country.

Western Armies, under Eisenhower's command, rounded up an estimated five million anti-communist refugees and delivered them to the Soviets who tortured them, sent them to slave camps, or murdered them.

All of this occurred because we refused to do what would have been easy for us to do—and what our top leaders had agreed just 17 months before that we must do: that is, take and hold Berlin and surrounding territory until postwar peace treaties were made.

Who made the decisions to pull our armies back in Europe and let the Soviets take over? General Eisenhower gave the orders; and, in his book, Crusade in Europe (published in 1948, before the awful consequences of those decisions were fully known to the public), Eisenhower took his share of credit for making the decisions. When he entered politics four years later, Eisenhower denied responsibility: he claimed that he was merely a soldier, obeying orders, implementing decisions which Presidents Roosevelt and Truman had made.

Memoirs of British military men indicate that Eisenhower went far beyond the call of military duty in his "co-operative" efforts to help the Soviets capture political prisoner's and enslave all of central Europe. Triumph in the West, by Arthur Bryant, published in 1959 by Doubleday & Company, as a "History of the War Years Based on the Diaries of Field-Marshal Lord Alanbrooke, Chief of the Imperial General Staff," reveals that, in the closing days of the war, General Eisenhower was often in direct communication with Stalin, reporting his decisions and actions to the Soviet dictator before Eisenhower's own military superiors knew what was going on.

Regardless of what responsibility General Eisenhower may or may not have had for formulating the decisions which held our armies back from Eastern Europe, those decisions seem to have stemmed from the conferences which Roosevelt had with Stalin at Tehran in 1943 and at Yalta in 1945.

* * * * *

But who made the decision to isolate Berlin 110 miles deep inside communist-controlled territory without any agreements concerning access routes by which the Western Powers could get to the city? According to Arthur Krock, of the New York Times, George F. Kennan, (a member of the Council on Foreign Relations) persuaded Roosevelt to accept the Berlin zoning arrangement. Kennan, at the time, was political adviser to Ambassador John G. Winant, who was the United States Representative on the three-member European Advisory Commission.

Mr. Krock's account (in the New York Times, June 18, 1961 and July 2, 1961) is rather involved; but here is the essence of it:

> President Roosevelt and Prime Minister Churchill agreed to enclose Berlin 110 miles within the Soviet occupation zone. Winant submitted a recommendation, embracing this agreement. Winant felt that it would offend the Soviets if we asked for guaranteed access routes, and believed that guarantees were unnecessary anyway. When submitting his recommendation to Washington, however, Winant attached a map on which a specific allied corridor of access into the city was drawn.
>
> Winant's proposal was never acted on in Washington. Therefore, the British submitted a recommendation. Roosevelt rejected the British plan, and made his own proposal. The British and Soviets disliked Roosevelt's plan; and negotiations over the zoning of Berlin were deadlocked.
>
> George F. Kennan broke the deadlock by going directly to Roosevelt and persuading him to accept the Berlin zoning agreement, which Mr. Krock calls a "war-breeding monstrosity," and a "witless travesty on statecraft and military competence."

Mr. Krock says most of his information came from one of Philip E. Mosely's articles in an old issue of Foreign Affairs—which I have been unable to get for my files. I cannot, therefore, guarantee the authenticity of Mr. Krock's account; but I can certainly agree with his conclusion that only Joseph Stalin and international communism benefitted from the "incredible zoning agreements" that placed "Berlin 110 miles within the Soviet zone and reserved no guaranteed access routes to the city from the British and American zones."

It is interesting to note that Philip E. Mosely (CFR member who was Cordell Hull's adviser when the postwar division of Germany was first discussed at the Moscow Conference in 1943) succeeded George F. Kennan as political adviser to John G. Winant of the European Advisory Commission shortly after Kennan had persuaded Roosevelt to accept the Berlin zoning agreements.

* * * * *

It is easy to see why the Soviets wanted the Berlin arrangement which Roosevelt gave them. It is not difficult to see the British viewpoint: squeezed between the two giants who were his allies, Churchill tried to play the Soviets against the Americans, in the interest of getting the most he could for the future trade and commerce of England.

But why would any American want (or, under any conditions, agree to) the crazy Berlin agreement? There are only three possible answers:

(1) the Americans who set up the Berlin arrangement—which means, specifically, George F. Kennan and Philip E. Mosely, representing the Council on Foreign Relations—were ignorant fools; or

(2) they wanted to make Berlin a powder keg which the Soviets could use, at will, to intimidate the West; or

(3) they wanted a permanent, ready source of war which the United States government could use, at any time, to salvage its own internationalist policies from criticism at home, by scaring the American people into "buckling down" and "tightening up" for "unity" behind our "courageous President" who is "calling the Kremlin bluff" by spending to prepare this nation for all-out war, if necessary, to "defend the interests of the free-world" in Berlin.

47

George F. Kennan and Philip E. Mosely and the other men associated with them in the Council on Foreign Relations are not ignorant fools. I do not believe they are traitors who wanted to serve the interests of the Kremlin. So, in trying to assess their motives, I am left with one choice: they wanted to set Berlin up as a perpetual excuse for any kind of program which the Council on Foreign Relations might want the American government to adopt.

Long, long ago, King Henry of England told Prince Hal that the way to run a country and keep the people from being too critical of how you run it, is to busy giddy minds with foreign quarrels.

A study of President Kennedy's July 25, 1961, speech to the nation about Berlin, together with an examination of the spending program which he recommended to Congress a few hours later, plus a review of contemporary accounts of how the stampeded Congress rushed to give the President all he asked–such a study, set against the backdrop of our refusal to do anything vigorous with regard to the communist menace in Cuba, will, I think, justify my conclusions as to the motives of men, still in power, who created the Berlin situation.

CHAPTER 3.

FPA–WORLD AFFAIRS COUNCIL–IPR

Through many interlocking organizations, the Council on Foreign Relations "educates" the public–and brings pressures upon Congress–to support CFR policies. All organizations, in this incredible propaganda web, work in their own way toward the objective of the Council on Foreign Relations: to create a one-world socialist system and to make America a part of it. All of the organizations have federal tax-exemption as "educational" groups; and they are all financed, in part, by tax-exempt foundations, the principal ones being Ford, Rockefeller, and Carnegie. Most of them also have close working relations with official agencies of the United States Government.

The CFR does not have formal affiliation–and can therefore disclaim official connection with–its subsidiary propaganda agencies (except the Committees on Foreign Relations, organized by the CFR in 30 cities throughout the United States); but the real and effective interlock between all these groups can be shown not only by their common objective (one-world socialism) and a common source of income (the foundations), but also by the overlapping of personnel: directors and officials of the Council on Foreign Relations are also officials in the interlocking organizations.

* * * * *

The Foreign Policy Association-World Affairs Center, 345 East 46th Street, New York 17, New York, is probably the most influential of all the agencies which can be shown as propaganda affiliates of the Council on Foreign Relations in matters concerned primarily with American foreign policy.

On April 29, 1960, the March-April Term Grand Jury of Fulton County, Georgia, handed down a Presentment concerning subversive materials in schools, which said:

"An extensive investigation has been made by the Jury into the Foreign Policy Association of New York City and its 'Great Decisions Program,' which it is sponsoring in our area . . .

"This matter was brought to our attention by the Americanism Committee of the Waldo M. Slaton Post 140, American Legion, and several other local patriotic groups. We were informed that the Great Decisions Program was being taught in our public high schools and by various well-meaning civic and religious groups, who were not aware of the past records of the leaders of the Foreign Policy Association, nor of the authors of the textbooks prescribed for this Great Decisions program.

"Evidence was presented to us showing that some of these leaders and authors had a long record, dating back many years, in which they either belonged to, or actively supported left-wing or subversive organizations.

"We further found that invitations to participate in these 'study groups' were being mailed throughout our county under the name of one of our local universities . . . We learned that the prescribed booklets were available upon request in our local public libraries . . .

"The range of the activity by this organization has reached alarming proportions in the schools and civic groups in certain other areas in Georgia. Its spread is a matter of deep concern to this Jury and we, therefore, call upon all school officials throughout the state to be particularly alert to this insidious and subversive material. We further recommend that all textbook committee members–city, county and state–recognize the undesirable features of this material and take action to remove it from our schools.

"Finally, we urge that all Grand Juries throughout the State of Georgia give matters of this nature their serious consideration."

On June 30, 1960, the May-June Term Grand Jury of Fulton County, Georgia, handed down another Presentment, which said:

"It is our understanding that the Foreign Policy Association's Great Decisions program, criticized by the March-April Grand Jury, Fulton County, has been removed from the Atlanta and Fulton County schools . . .

"Numerous letters from all over the United States have been received by this grand jury, from individuals and associations, commending the Presentment of the previous grand jury on the Foreign Policy Association. Not a single letter has been received by us criticizing these presentments."

In September, 1960, the Americanism Committee of Waldo M. Slaton Post No. 140, The American Legion, 3905 Powers Ferry Road, N.W., Atlanta 5, Georgia, published a 112-page mimeographed book entitled The Truth About the Foreign Policy Association (available directly from the Post at $1.00 per copy). In the Foreword to this book, the Americanism Committee says:

"How can we account for our apathetic acceptance of the presence of this arch-murderer (Khrushchev, during his tour of the United States at Eisenhower's invitation) in America? What has so dulled our sense of moral values that we could look on without revulsion while he was being wined and dined by our officials? How could we dismiss with indifference the shameful spectacle of these officials posing for pictures with this grinning Russian assassin–pictures which we knew he would use to prove to communism's enslaved populations that the Americans are no longer their friends, but the friends of Khrushchev?

"There is only one explanation for this lapse from the Americanism of former days: we are being brainwashed into the belief that we can safely do business with communism–brainwashed by an interlocked group of so-called 'educational' organizations offering 'do-it-yourself' courses which pretend to instruct the public in the intricacies of foreign policy, but which actually mask clever propaganda operations designed to sell 'co-existence' to Americans. There are many of these propaganda outfits working to undermine Americans' faith in America, but none, in our opinion, is as slick or as smooth or as dangerous as the Foreign Policy Association of Russian-born Vera Micheles Dean . . .

"This documented handbook has been prepared in response to numerous requests for duplicates of the file which formed the basis of the case (before the Fulton County Grand Juries) against the Foreign Policy Association. We hope that it will assist patriots everywhere in resisting the un-American propaganda of the Red China appeasers, the pro-Soviet apologists, the relativists, and other dangerous propagandists who are weakening Americans' sense of honor and their will to survive."

The Truth About The Foreign Policy Association sets out the communist front record of Vera Micheles Dean (who was Research Director of the FPA until shortly after the Legion Post made this exposure, when she resigned amidst almost-tearful words of praise and farewell on the part of FPA-WAC officials). The Legion Post booklet sets out the communist front records of various other persons connected with the FPA; it presents and analyzes several publications of the FPA,

52

including materials used in the Great Decisions program; it reveals that FPA establishes respectability and public acceptance for itself by publicizing "endorsements" of prominent Americans; it shows that many of the FPA's claims of endorsements are false; it shows the interlocking connections and close working relationships between the Foreign Policy Association and other organizations, particularly the National Council of Churches; and it presents a great deal of general documentation on FPA's activities, operations, and connections.

The Foreign Policy Association was organized in 1918 and incorporated under the laws of New York in 1928 (the Council on Foreign Relations was organized in 1919 and incorporated in 1921). Rockefeller and Carnegie money was responsible for both FPA and CFR becoming powerful organizations.

The late U. S. Congressman Louis T. McFadden (Pennsylvania), as early as 1934, said that the Foreign Policy Association, working in close conjunction with a comparable British group, was formed, largely under the aegis of Felix Frankfurter and Paul Warburg, to promote a "planned" or socialist economy in the United States, and to integrate the American system into a worldwide socialist system. Warburg and Frankfurter (early CFR members) were among the many influential persons who worked closely with Colonel Edward M. House, father of the Council on Foreign Relations.

* * * * *

From its early days, the Foreign Policy Association had interlocking personnel, and worked in close co-operation with the Institute of Pacific Relations, which was formed in 1925 as a tax-exempt educational organization, and which was financed by the great foundations—and by the same groups of businessmen and corporations which have always financed the CFR and the FPA.

The IPR played a more important role than any other American organization in shaping public opinion and influencing official American policy with regard to Asia.

For more than twenty years, the IPR influenced directly or indirectly the selection of Far Eastern scholars for important teaching posts in colleges and universities—and the selection of officials for posts concerning Asia in the State Department. The IPR publications were standard materials in most American colleges, in thirteen hundred public school systems, and in the armed forces; and millions of IPR publications were distributed to all these institutions.

Along toward the end of World War II, there were rumblings that the powerful IPR might be a communist front, despite its respectable façade—despite the fact that a great majority of its members were Americans whose patriotism and integrity were beyond question.

* * * * *

In 1951, the Senate Internal Security Subcommittee, under the chairmanship of the late Pat McCarran (Democrat, Nevada) began an investigation which lasted many months and became the most important, careful, and productive investigation ever conducted by a committee of Congress.

The McCarran investigation of the IPR was predicated on the assumption that United States diplomacy had never suffered a more disastrous defeat than in its failure to avert the communist conquest of China.

The communist conquest of China led to the Korean war; and the tragic mishandling of this war on the part of Washington and United Nations officialdom destroyed American prestige throughout Asia, and built Chinese communist military power into a menacing colossus.

The Senate investigation revealed that the American policy decisions which produced these disastrous consequences were made by IPR officials who were traitors, or under the influence of traitors, whose allegiance lay in Moscow.

Owen Lattimore, guiding light of the IPR during its most important years (and also a member of the Council on Foreign Relations), was termed a conscious articulate instrument of the Soviet international conspiracy.

Alger Hiss (a CFR member who was later identified as a Soviet spy) was closely tied in with the IPR during his long and influential career in government service. Hiss became a trustee of the IPR after his resignation from the State Department. The secret information which Hiss delivered to a Soviet spy ring in the 1930's kept the Soviets apprised of American activity in the Far East.

Lauchlin Currie (also a member of the CFR) was an administrative assistant to President Roosevelt. Harry Dexter White virtually ran the Treasury Department under both Roosevelt and Truman. Both Currie and White had strong connections with the IPR; and both were Soviet spies–who not only channeled important American secrets to Soviet military intelligence, but also influenced and formulated American policies to suit the Soviets.

By the time the McCarran investigation ended, the whole nation knew that the IPR was, as the McCarran committee had characterized it, a transmission belt for Soviet propaganda in the United States.

The IPR, thoroughly discredited, had lost its power and influence; but its work was carried on, without any perceptible decline in effectiveness, by the Foreign Policy Association.

* * * * *

The FPA did this job through its Councils on World Affairs, which had been set up in key cities throughout the United States.

These councils are all "anti-communist." They include among their members the business, financial, social, cultural, and educational leaders

55

of the community. Their announced purpose is to help citizens become better informed on international affairs and foreign policy. To this end, they arrange public discussion groups, forums, seminars in connection with local schools and colleges, radio-television programs, and lecture series. They distribute a mammoth quantity of expensively produced material–to schools, civic clubs, discussion groups, and so on, at little or no cost.

The Councils bring world-renowned speakers to their community. Hence, Council events generally make headlines and get wide coverage on radio and television. The Foreign Policy Associations' Councils on World Affairs, through the parent organization, through the Council on Foreign Relations, and through a multitude of other channels, have close working relationships with the State Department.

Hence, many of the distinguished speakers whom the Councils present are handpicked by the State Department; and they travel (sometimes from distant foreign lands) at United States taxpayers' expense.

To avert criticism (or to provide themselves with ammunition against criticism when it arises) that they are nothing but internationalist propaganda agencies, the Councils on World Affairs distribute a little literature which, and present a few speakers who, give the general appearance of being against the internationalist program of one-world socialism. But their anti-internationalism presentations are generally milk-and-water middle-of-the-roadism which is virtually meaningless. Most Councils-on-World-Affairs presentations give persuasive internationalist propaganda.

Thus, the Foreign Policy Association, through its Councils on World Affairs–and another affiliated activity, the Great Decisions program–has managed to enroll some "conservative" community leadership into an effective propaganda effort for one-world socialism.

The World Affairs Center was set up with national headquarters at 345 East 46th Street in New York City, as a formal affiliate of the Foreign Policy Association, to handle the important job of directing the various "independent" Councils on World Affairs, located in major cities throughout the nation. In March, 1960, the FPA merged with the World Affairs Center to form one organization: the Foreign Policy Association-World Affairs Center.

* * * * *

The FPA-WAC describes its Great Decisions program as an annual nation-wide review, by local groups under local sponsorship, of problems affecting United States Foreign Policy. FPA-WAC provides Fact Sheet Kits, which contain reading material for these local discussion groups. These kits present what FPA calls a "common fund of information" for all participants. They also provide an "opinion" ballot which permits each participant, at the end of the Great Decisions discussion program, to register his viewpoint and send it to officials in Washington.

The old IPR line (fostering American policies which helped communists take over China) was that the Chinese communists were not communists at all but democratic "agrarian reformers" whom the Chinese people loved and respected, and whom the Chinese people were going to install as the rulers of new China, regardless of what America did; and that, therefore, it was in our best interest to be friendly with these "agrarian reformers" so that China would remain a friendly power once the "reformers" took over.

A major objective of the FPA-WAC—since it fell heir to the work of the IPR—is to foster American diplomatic recognition of red China.

The FPA-WAC, and its subordinate Councils on World Affairs, do this propaganda job most cleverly. Most FPA spokesmen (except a few like Cyrus Eaton, who is a darling of the FPA and occasionally writes for its publications) are "anti-communists" who admit that the Chinese communists are real communists. They admit that it is not pleasant (in the wake of our memories of Korea) to think of extending diplomatic recognition to red China; and they do not always openly advocate such a move; but their literature and Great Decisions operations and other activities all subtly inculcate the idea that, however much we may dislike the Chinese communists, it is highly probable that we can best promote American interests by "eventually" recognizing red China.

In this connection, the FPA-WAC Great Decisions program for 1957 was especially interesting. One question posed that year was "Should U. S. Deal With Red China?" Discussion of this topic was divided into four corollary questions: Why Two Chinas? What are Red China's goals? Does Red China threaten 'uncommitted' Asia? Red China's record—what U. S. Policy?

The FPA-WAC Fact Sheet Kit, which sets out background information for the "study" and "voting" on the red China question, contains nothing that would remind Americans of Chinese communist atrocities against our men in Korea or in any way make Americans really angry at the communists. In the discussion of the "two Chinas," the communists sound somewhat more attractive than the nationalists. In the discussion of red China's "goals," there is nothing about the communist goal of enslaving all Asia; there are simply statistics showing how much more progress red China has made than "democratic" India—with less outside help than "democratic" India has received from the United States.

In the discussion of whether red China threatens the rest of Asia, the FPA-WAC material makes no inference that the reds are an evil, aggressive power—but it does let the reader know that the reds in China are a mighty military power that we must reckon with, in realistic terms. Nothing is said in the FPA-WAC Fact Sheet Kit about the communist rape of Tibet. Rather, one gets the impression that Tibet is a normal, traditional province of China which has now returned to the homeland.

After studying the problems of communist China from this FPA-WAC "Fact Sheet," Great Decisions participants were given an opportunity to cast an "Opinion Ballot" on the four specific questions posed. The "Opinions" were already written out on the FPA-WAC ballot. The voter had only to select the opinion he liked best, and mark it. Here are the five choices of opinions given voters on the Foreign Policy Association's Great Decisions 1957 Opinion Ballot, concerning U. S. diplomatic recognition of red China.

"a. Recognize Peiping now, because we can deal with Far East political and other problems more easily if we have diplomatic relations with Peiping.
"b. Go slow on recognizing them but agree to further talks and, if progress is made, be willing to grant recognition at some future date.
"c. Refuse to recognize them under any circumstances.
"d. Acknowledge that the Peiping government is the effective government of China (recognition de facto) and deal with it as much as seems useful, on this basis, but avoid full diplomatic relations for the present.
"e. Other."

* * * * *

General purposes of the Foreign Policy Association-World Affairs Center are rather well indicated in a fund-raising letter, mailed to American businessmen all over the nation, on February 23, 1961. The letter was on the letterhead of Consolidated Foods Corporation, 135 South La Salle Street, Chicago 3, Illinois, and was signed by Nathan Cummings, Chairman of the Board. Here is a part of Mr. Cummings' appeal to other businessmen to contribute money to the FPA-WAC:

"In his inaugural address which I had the privilege of personally hearing in Washington, President Kennedy summoned the American people to responsibility in foreign policy: . . .

"This call for individual initiative by the President characterizes the kind of citizen responsibility in world affairs which the Foreign

Policy Association-World Affairs Center has been energetically trying to build since its founding in 1918 . . .

"The FPA-WAC's national program for informing the American public of the urgent matters of foreign policy such as those mentioned by the President—'the survival and the success of liberty,' 'inspection and control of arms,' the forging of 'a grand and global alliance' to 'assure a more fruitful life for all mankind'— is making remarkable progress.

"The enclosed 'Memorandum: 1960-61' describes the program and past achievement of this 42-year-old organization. Particularly worthy of mention is their annual 'Great Decisions' program which last year engaged more than a quarter of a million Americans in eight weeks of discussion of U. S. foreign policy and reached hundreds of thousands of others with related radio, television and newspaper background programs and articles on these important topics.

"Of the basic budget for 1960-61 of $1,140,700, nearly one-third must be raised from individual and corporate sources to meet minimal operating needs. The fact that over 400 major corporations, some of whom contribute as much as $5,000, already support FPA-WAC is evidence of the effectiveness and vitality of its educational program . . .

"I hope that you and your company will join ours in generously supporting this work."

Erwin D. Canham, editor of The Christian Science Monitor, has caustically denounced the American Legion Post in Atlanta for its "attack" on the FPA.

Mr. Canham, in a letter dated April 25, 1961, accused the American Legion Post of making a "completely false" statement when the Post contended that Mr. Canham and the Monitor advocated the seating of red China in the UN. Mr. Canham said:

"This newspaper's editorial policy has never espoused any such position."

I have in my file a letter which Mr. Canham wrote, April 29, 1960, as editor of The Christian Science Monitor, on the Monitor's letterhead. In this letter, Mr. Canham says:

"I believe that the United States should open diplomatic relations with communist China."

The interesting thing here is the coincidence of Mr. Canham's policy with regard to red China, and the policy of the Foreign Policy Association-World Affairs Center.

The Great Decisions program for 1957 (discussed above) was obviously intended to lead Americans to acceptance of U. S. diplomatic recognition of red China. The same material, however, made it clear that the invisible government was not yet advocating the seating of red China in the UN! Do these backstairs formulators and managers of United States opinion and governmental policies have more respect for the UN than they have for the US? Or, do they fear that bringing red China into the UN (before U. S. recognition) would finish discrediting that already discredited organization and cause the American people to demand American withdrawal?

Christian Scientists (through Mr. Canham and the Monitor), Protestants (through the National Council of Churches), Quakers (through the American Friends Service Committee), and Jews (through the American Jewish Committee, The Anti-Defamation League, and other organizations) are among the religious groups which have publicly supported activities of the Foreign Policy Association. Powerful Catholic personalities and publications have endorsed FPA work, too.

On December 9, 1959, The Right Rev. Timothy F. O'Leary, Superintendent of Catholic Schools for the Archdiocese of Boston, wrote to all Catholic schools in the district, telling them that he was making plans for their participation with the World Affairs Council and the Foreign Policy Association in the Great Decisions 1960 Program.

On November 27, 1960, Our Sunday Visitor (largest and perhaps most influential Catholic newspaper in America) featured an article by Frank Folsom, Chairman of the Executive Committee of the Board of Directors of the Radio Corporation of America, and a leading Catholic layman. Mr. Folsom was effusive in his praise of the FPA-WAC Great Decisions program.

*　*　*　*　*

The interlock between the Council on Foreign Relations and the Foreign Policy Association-World Affairs Center can be seen in the list of officers and directors of the FPA-WAC:

Eustace Seligman, Chairman of the FPA-WAC, is a partner in Sullivan and Cromwell, the law firm of the late John Foster Dulles, a leading CFR member.

John W. Nason, President of FPA-WAC, is a member of the Council on Foreign Relations.

Walter H. Wheeler, Jr., President of Pitney-Bowes, Inc., is Vice Chairman of FPA-WAC, and also a member of the CFR.

Gerald F. Beal, of the J. Henry Schroeder Banking Corporation of New York, is Treasurer of FPA-WAC, and also a member of the Council on Foreign Relations.

Mrs. Andrew G. Carey is Secretary of FPA-WAC. Her husband is a member of the CFR.

Emile E. Soubry, Executive Vice President and Director of the Standard Oil Company of New Jersey, is Chairman of the Executive Committee of FPA-WAC, and also a member of the CFR.

Benjamin J. Buttenwieser, of Kuhn, Loeb, and Company, in New York, is a member of the Executive Committee of FPA-WAC, and also a member of the CFR.

Joseph E. Johnson (old friend of Alger Hiss, who succeeded Hiss as President of the Carnegie Endowment for International Peace) is a member of the Executive Committee of the FPA-WAC, and also a member of the CFR.

Harold F. Linder, Vice Chairman of the General American Investors Company, is a member of the Executive Committee of FPA-WAC, and also a member of the CFR.

A. William Loos, Executive Director of the Church Peace Union, is a member of the Executive Committee of the FPA-WAC. Mr. Loos attended the CFR meeting with high communist party officials in the Soviet Union in May, 1961.

Henry Siegbert, formerly a partner in the investment banking firm of Adolph Lewisohn & Sons, is a member of the Executive Committee of the FPA-WAC, and also a member of the CFR.

CHAPTER 4.

COMMITTEE FOR ECONOMIC DEVELOPMENT

On June 20, 1961, The San Francisco Examiner published a United Press International news story with a June 19, Washington, D. C. date line, under the headline "J.F.K. Backs Tax Cut Plan."

Here are portions of the article:

"President Kennedy today urged Congress and the people to give a close study to a monetary reform proposal which would empower him to cut income taxes in recession periods.

"He issued the statement after receiving a bulky report from the Commission of Money and Credit . . .

"The 27-member commission was set up in 1957 by the Committee for Economic Development (CED). Its three-year study was financed by $1.3 million in grants from the CED and the Ford and Merrill Foundation.

"One of the key recommendations was to give the President limited power to cut the 20 percent tax rate on the first $2000 of personal income, if needed to help the economy . . .

"The report also recommended extensive changes in the Federal Reserve System, set up in 1913 as the core of the Nation's banking system . . ."

This San Francisco Examiner article is a classic example of propaganda disguised as straight news reporting.

* * * * *

A story about the President supporting a plan for reducing taxes could not fail to command sympathetic attention. But the truth is that the tax reform proposals of the Commission on Money and Credit would give the President as much power and leeway to raise taxes as to lower them.

In its 282-page report, the Commission made 87 separate proposals. One would permit the President (on his own initiative) to reduce the basic income-tax rate (the one that applies to practically every person who has any income at all) from 20% to 15%. It would also permit the President to raise the basic rate from 20% to 25%.

The idea of giving the President such power is as alien to American political principles as communism itself is. The proposed "machinery" for granting such Presidential power would violate every basic principle of our constitutional system. Under the Commission's proposal, the President would announce that he was going to increase or decrease taxes. If, within sixty days, Congress did not veto the plan, it would become law, effective for six months, at which time it would have to be renewed by the same procedure. That is very similar to the Soviet way. It could not be more foreign to the American way if it had been lifted from the Soviet constitution.

Other proposals in the report of the Commission on Money and Credit, filed on June 18, 1961, after a three-year study:

1. The Federal Reserve Act would be amended to give the President control over the Federal Reserve System—which, as set up in 1913, is supposed to be free of any kind of political control, from the White House or elsewhere.

65

2. The Commission recommends elimination of the legal requirement that the Federal Reserve System maintain a gold reserve as backing for American currency. A bill was introduced in Congress (May 9, 1961, by U. S. Congressman Abraham Multer, New York Democrat) to implement this Commission recommendation. The bill would take away from American citizens twelve billion dollars in gold which supports their own currency, and enable government to pour this gold out to foreigners, as long as it lasts, leaving Americans with a worthless currency, and at the mercy of foreign governments and bankers (see the Dan Smoot Report, "Gold and Treachery," May 22, 1961).

3. The banking laws of individual states would be ignored or invalidated: banking laws of 33 states prohibit mutual savings banks; the Commission on Money and Credit wants a federal law to permit such banks in all states.

4. The Commission would circumvent, if not eliminate, state laws governing the insurance industry: the Commission proposes a federal law which would permit insurance companies to obtain federal charters and claim federal, rather than state, regulation.

5. The Commission would subject all private pension funds to federal supervision.

6. The Commission would abolish congressional limitations on the size of the national debt—so that the debt could go as high as the President pleased, without any interference from Congress.

7. The Commission recommends that Congress approve all federal public works projects three years in advance, so that the President could order the projects when he felt the economy needed stimulation.

Remembering how President Kennedy and his administrative officials and congressional leaders used political extortion and promises of bribes with public money to force the House of Representatives, in January, 1961, to pack the House Rules Committee, imagine how the President could whip Congress, and the whole nation, into line if the President had just some of the additional, unconstitutional power which the Commission on Money and Credit wants him to have.

* * * * *

The objective of the Commission on Money and Credit (to finish the conversion of America into a total socialist state, under the dictatorship of whatever "proletarian" happens to be enthroned in the White House) can be seen, between the lines, in the Commission's remarks about the "formidable problem" of unemployment.

The Commission wants unemployment to drop to the point where the number of jobless workers will equal the number of vacant jobs! And the clear implication is that the federal government must adopt whatever policies necessary to create this condition.

Such a condition can exist only in a slave system—like the socialist system of communist China where, for example, all "farmers" (men, women, and children) enjoy full employment; under the whips of overseers, on the collective farms of communism.

The Commission on Money and Credit was created on November 21, 1957, by the Committee for Economic Development (CED). In the 1957 Annual Report of the CED, Mr. Donald K. David, CED Chairman, gave the history of the Commission on Money and Credit. Mr. David said:

> "CED began nine years ago [1948] to call attention to the need for a comprehensive reassessment of our entire system of money and credit.
>
> "When the last such survey of the economic scene was made by the Aldrich Commission in 1911, we had no central banking system, no guaranteed deposits or guaranteed mortgages. There

were no personal or corporate income taxes; no group insurance plans, pension funds, or Social Security system . . .

"Although CED had envisaged a commission created by government, the inability of government to obtain the consensus required for launching the study became as apparent as the need for avoiding further delay. So, after receiving encouragement from other research institutions, leaders in Congress, the Administration, and from various leaders in private life, CED's Trustees decided to sponsor the effort, assisted by a grant from The Ford Foundation . . ."

Here is the membership of the CED's Commission on Money and Credit:

Frazar B. Wilde, Chairman (President of Connecticut General Life Insurance Company)

Hans Christian Sonne, Vice-Chairman (New York; official in numerous foundations and related organizations, such as Twentieth Century Fund; American-Scandanavian Foundation; National Planning Association; and so on)

Adolf A. Berle, Jr. (New York; Berle has been in and out of important posts in government for many years; he is an anti-communist socialist; he resigned from the Commission on Money and Credit to accept his present job handling Latin American affairs in the State Department)

James B. Black (Chairman of the Board of Pacific Gas and Electric Company)

Marriner S. Eccles (Chairman of the Board of the First Security Corporation; formerly Assistant to the Secretary of the Treasury under Roosevelt; Governor of Federal Reserve Board; and official in numerous international banking organizations, such as the Export-Import Bank)

Lamar Fleming, Jr. (Chairman of the Board of Anderson, Clayton & Co., Houston, Texas)

Henry H. Fowler (Washington, D.C.; resigned from the Commission on February 3 to accept appointment from Kennedy as Under Secretary of the Treasury)

Gaylord A. Freeman, Jr. (President of the First National Bank, Chicago)

Philip M. Klutznick (Park Forest, Ill., resigned from the Commission on February 8, to accept appointment from President Kennedy as United States Representative to the United Nations Economic and Social Council)

Fred Lazarus, Jr. (Chairman of the Board of Federated Department Stores, Inc.)

Isador Lubin (Professor of Public Affairs at Rutgers University)

J. Irwin Miller (Chairman of the Board of Cummins Engine Company)

Robert R. Nathan (Washington, D.C.; has been in and out of many important government jobs since the first Roosevelt Administration)

Emil Rieve (President emeritus of the Textile Workers Union–AFL-CIO)

David Rockefeller (President of Chase Manhattan Bank)

Stanley H. Ruttenberg (Research Director for AFL-CIO)

Charles Sawyer (Cincinnati lawyer, prominent in Democratic Party politics in Ohio)

Earl B. Schwulst (President of the Bowery Savings Bank in New York)

Charles B. Shuman (President of the American Farm Bureau Federation)

Jesse W. Tapp (Chairman of the Board, Bank of America)

John Cameron Thomson (former Chairman of the Board of Northwest Bancorporation, Minneapolis)

Willard L. Thorp (Director of the Merrill Center for Economics at Amherst College)

Theodore O. Yntema (Vice President in Charge of Finance, Ford Motor Company)

William F. Schnitzler (Secretary-Treasurer of AFL-CIO; resigned from the Commission in 1960)

Joseph M., Dodge (Chairman of the Board of Detroit Bank and Trust Co.; resigned from the Commission in 1960)

Beardsley Ruml (well-known and influential new deal economist who held numerous posts with foundations and related organizations; is sometimes called the father of the federal withholding tax law, enacted during World War II; Dr. Ruml died before the Commission on Money and Credit completed its report)

Fred T. Greene (President of the Home Loan Bank of Indianapolis; died before the Commission completed its report)

The director of research for the Commission Was Dr. Bertrand Fox, professor at the Harvard Graduate School of Business Administration. His assistant was Dr. Eli Shapiro, Professor of Finance at the Massachusetts Institute of Technology.

Of the 27 persons who served as members of the Commission on Money and Credit, 13 (Wilde, Sonne, Berle, Fleming, Fowler, Lubin, Nathan, Rockefeller, Tapp, Thorp, Yntema, Dodge, Ruml) were members of the Council on Foreign Relations.

In other words, the Commission on Money and Credit was just another tax-exempt propaganda agency of America's invisible government, the Council on Foreign Relations.

* * * * *

The above discussion of the Commission on Money and Credit, together with the roster of membership, was first published in The Dan Smoot Report dated July 3, 1961.

On September 22, 1961, Mr. Charles B. Shuman, President of the American Farm Bureau Federation, wrote me a letter, saying:

"I was a member of the Commission on Money and Credit but you will notice that I filed very strong objections to several of the recommendations which you brought to the attention of your readers. I do not agree with the Commission recommendations to authorize the President of the United States to vary the rate of income tax. Neither do I agree that the gold reserve requirement should be abandoned. I agree with several of your criticisms of the Report but I cannot agree that 'the objective of the Commission on Money and Credit (to finish the conversion of America into a total socialist state, under the dictatorship of whatever proletarian happens to be enthroned in the White House) can be seen, between the lines, in the Commission's remarks about the formidable problem of unemployment.'

"At its worst, it was a compromise of the divergent viewpoint of the conservative and liberal members of the Commission."

I will not argue with Mr. Shuman, an honest and honorable man, about the objective of the Commission; but I will reassert the obvious: recommendations of the Commission on Money and Credit, if fully implemented, would finish the conversion of America into a total socialist state.

* * * * *

As pointed out before, the various agencies which interlock with the Council on Foreign Relations do not have formal affiliation with the

71

Council, or generally, with each other; but their effective togetherness is revealed by their unanimity of purpose: They are all working toward the ultimate objective of creating a one-world socialist system and making America a part of it.

This ambitious scheme was first conceived and put into operation, during the administrations of Woodrow Wilson, by Colonel Edward M. House, and by the powerful international bankers whom House influenced.

House founded the Council on Foreign Relations for the purpose of creating (and conditioning the American people to accept) what House called a "positive" foreign policy for America–a policy which would entwine the affairs of America with those of other nations until this nation would be sucked into a world-government arrangement.

Colonel House knew, however, that America could not become a province in a one-world socialist system unless America's economy was first socialized. Consequently, House laid the groundwork for "positive" domestic policies of government too–policies which could gradually place government in control of the nation's economy until, before the public realized what was happening, we would already have a socialist dictatorship.

The following passages are from pages 152-157 of The Intimate Papers of Colonel House:

"The extent of Colonel House's influence upon the legislative plans of the Administration [Wilson's] may be gathered from a remarkable document ... In the autumn of 1912, immediately after the presidential election [when Wilson was elected for his first term] there was published a novel, or political romance, entitled Philip Dru: Administrator.

"It was the story of a young West Point graduate ... who was caught by the spirit of revolt against the tyranny of privileged interests. A stupid and reactionary government at Washington provokes armed rebellion, in which Dru joins whole-heartedly and which he ultimately leads to complete success. He himself becomes a dictator and proceeds by ordinance to remake the mechanism of government, to reform the basic laws that determine the relation of the classes, to remodel the defensive forces of the republic, and to bring about an international grouping or league of powers . . .

"Five years after its publication, an enterprising bookseller, noting the growing influence of House in the Wilson Administration, wrote with regard to the book: 'As time goes on the interest in it becomes more intense, due to the fact that so many of the ideas expressed by Philip Dru: Administrator, have become laws of this Republic, and so many of his ideas have been discussed as becoming laws . . . Is Colonel E. M. House of Texas the author?' . . .

"Colonel House was, in truth, the author . . .

"'Philip Dru' . . . gives us an insight into the main political and social principles that actuated House in his companionship with President Wilson. Through it runs the note of social democracy reminiscent of Louis Blanc and the revolutionaries of 1848 . . .

"Through the book also runs the idea that in the United States, government is unresponsive to popular desires–a 'negative' government, House calls it . . .

"The specific measures enacted by Philip Dru as Administrator of the nation, indicated the reforms desired by House.

"The Administrator appointed a 'board composed of economists . . . who . . . were instructed to work out a tariff law which would contemplate the abolition of the theory of protection as a governmental policy.'

"'The Administrator further directed the tax board to work out a graduated income tax . . .

"Philip Dru also provided for the 'formulation of a new banking law, affording a flexible currency bottomed largely upon commercial assets . . . He also proposed making corporations share with the government and states a certain part of their earnings . . .

"'Labor is no longer to be classed as an inert commodity to be bought and sold by the law of supply and demand.'

"Dru 'prepared an old age pension law and also a laborer's insurance law . . . '

"'He had incorporated in the Franchise Law the right of Labor to have one representative upon the boards of corporations and to share a certain percentage of the earnings above the wages, after a reasonable percent upon the capital had been earned. In turn, it was to be obligatory upon them (the laborers) not to strike, but to submit all grievances to arbitration.'"

Need it be pointed out that "Louis Blanc and the revolutionaries of 1848," on whom Colonel House patterned his plan for remaking America, had a scheme for the world virtually identical with that of Karl Marx and Frederick Engles—those socialist revolutionaries who wrote the Communist Manifesto in 1848?

* * * * *

In 1918, Franklin K. Lane, Woodrow Wilson's Secretary of the Interior, in a private letter, wrote, concerning the influence of 'Philip Dru' on President Wilson:

"All that book has said should be, comes about . . . The President comes to Philip Dru, in the end."

The end is a socialist dictatorship of the proletariat, identical with that which now exists in the Soviet Union. We have already "come to" a major portion of Colonel House's program for us. The unrealized portions of the program are now promises in the platforms of both our major political parties, they are in the legislative proposals of the Administration in power and of its leaders in Congress; they are the objectives of the Council on Foreign Relations, whose members occupy key posts in Government, from the Presidency downward, and who dominate a vast network of influential, tax-exempt "educational" agencies, whose role is to "educate" the Congress and the people to accept the total socialist program for America.

The Committee for Economic Development (which created the Commission on Money and Credit) is the major propaganda arm of the Council on Foreign Relations, in the important work of socializing the American economy.

* * * * *

Paul G. Hoffman is the father of CED. Hoffman, an influential member of the CFR, was formerly President of Studebaker Corp.; former President of Ford Foundation; Honorary Chairman of the Fund for the Republic; has held many powerful jobs in government since the days of Roosevelt; and is now Director of the Special United Nations Fund for Economic Development–SUNFED–the UN agency which is giving American tax money as economic aid to communist Castro in Cuba. Hoffman, in 1939, conceived the idea of setting up a tax-exempt "economic committee" which would prepare new economic policies for the nation and then prepare the public and Congress to accept them.

Hoffman founded the Committee for Economic Development in 1942. The organization was incorporated in September of that year, with Paul G. Hoffman as Chairman. Major offices in the Committee for Economic Development have always been occupied by members of the Council on Foreign Relations–persons who generally have important positions in many other interlocking organizations, in the foundations, in the big corporations which finance the great interlock, and/or in government.

* * * * *

Here are the Council on Foreign Relations members who joined Paul Hoffman in setting up the CED in 1942:

William Benton (former U.S. Senator, now Chairman of the Board of Encyclopaedia Britannica; former Assistant Secretary of State; Trustee and former Vice President, University of Chicago)

Will L. Clayton (founder of Anderson, Clayton & Co., Houston; former Assistant Secretary of Commerce and Under Secretary of State under Roosevelt and Truman; Eisenhower's National Security Training Commissioner)

Ralph E. Flanders (former United States Senator)

Marion B. Folsom (Eisenhower's Secretary of the Department of Health, Education, and Welfare; many other positions in the Roosevelt and Truman Administrations; Board of Overseers, Harvard)

Eric A. Johnston (former Director, Economic Stabilization Agency; many other positions in the Roosevelt-Truman-Eisenhower Administrations; former Director and President of U.S. Chamber of Commerce; now President of the Motion Picture Association of America)

Thomas B. McCabe (former Lend-Lease Administrator; former Chairman of the Board of Governors, Federal Reserve System; President of Scott Paper Company since 1927)

Harry Scherman (founder and Chairman of the Board, Book of the Month Club, Inc.)

* * * * *

Here are Council on Foreign Relations members who were Chairmen of the Committee for Economic Development from 1942 through 1959:

Paul G. Hoffman, 1942-48

Marion B. Folsom, 1950-53

Meyer Kestnbaum, 1953-55 (President, Hart Schaffner & Marx; Director, Fund for the Republic; Director, Chicago and Northwestern Railroad)

J. D. Zellerbach, 1955-57 (Eisenhower's Ambassador to Italy; President and Director of Crown-Zellerbach Corp.; Chairman of the Board and Director, Fibreboard Products, Inc.; Director, Wells Fargo Bank & Union Trust Co.)

Donald K. David, 1957-59 (Dean, Harvard University; Trustee of the Ford Foundation, Carnegie Institute, Merrill Foundation; Board of Directors, R. H. Macy & Co., General Electric Corp., First National City Bank of New York, Aluminum, Ltd., Ford Motor Co.)

Of the CED Board of Trustees listed in the CED's 1957 Annual Report, 47 were members of the Council on Foreign Relations.

* * * * *

The Research and Policy Committee of the Committee for Economic Development is the select inner-group which actually runs the CED. In 1957, the following members of the Research and Policy Committee were also members of the Council on Foreign Relations:

Frazar B. Wilde, Chairman

Frank Altschul (Chairman of the Board, General American Investors Corp.; Vice Chairman, National Planning Association; Vice President, Woodrow Wilson Foundation)

77

Don G. Mitchell (Chairman of the Board, Sylvania Electric Products, Inc.)

Alfred C. Neal (former official, Office of Price Administration; now member of the Board of Governors, Federal Reserve Bank of Boston; President of CED)

Howard C. Petersen (former council to Committee to Draft Selective Service Regulations; Assistant Secretary of War; now President, Philadelphia Trust Company; Trustee, Temple University)

Philip D. Reed (many positions in the Roosevelt and Truman Administrations; member, U. S. Delegation to UN Conference at San Francisco, 1945; now Chairman, Finance Committee, General Electric Co.; Director of Canadian General Electric Co., Bankers Trust Co., Metropolitan Life Insurance Co.)

Beardsley Ruml

Harry Scherman

Wayne Chatfield Taylor (many government positions including Assistant Secretary of Treasury, Under Secretary of Commerce; presently an economic adviser)

Theodore O. Yntema

* * * * *

In its annual report for 1957, the Committee for Economic Development boasted of some of its past accomplishments and its future plans.

Mr. Howard C. Petersen, Chairman of the CED's Subcommittee on Economic Development Assistance (and a member of the Council on Foreign Relations) said that his committee originated the idea of creating the Development Loan Fund, which was authorized by Congress in Section 6 of the Foreign Aid Bill of 1957, which Eisenhower established by Executive Order on December 13, 1957, and which may be the most sinister step ever taken by the internationalist foreign-aid lobby.

In 1956, when President Eisenhower requested an appropriation of $4,860,000,000 for foreign aid, he asked Congress to authorize foreign aid commitments for the next ten years. Congress refused the ten-year plan. In 1957, the internationalists' ideal of a permanent authorization for foreign aid was wrapped up in the Development Loan Fund scheme.

Only a few Congressmen raised any question about it. Below are passages taken from the Congressional Record of July 15, 1957, the day the Development Loan Fund was discussed in the House.

Congressman A. S. J. Carnahan (Democrat, Missouri) floor manager for the Foreign Aid Bill, rose to explain Section 6, which established the Development Loan Fund, saying:

"The United States, in order to provide effective assistance [to all underdeveloped countries of the world] . . . must have available a substantial fund upon which it can draw. The fund must be large enough so that all of the underdeveloped nations of the free world will feel that they will have an opportunity to participate in it.

"We cannot wisely say that we should make a small amount available the first year and see how things work out. If we are able to offer assistance only to the select few, we will inevitably antagonize many other countries whose future friendship and cooperation will be important to us . . . in addition to an initial authorization of an appropriation of $500 million, the bill includes authorization for borrowing from the Treasury $500 million beginning in fiscal 1959, and an additional $500 million beginning in fiscal 1960."

Thus, Congressman Carnahan, arguing for foreign aid, outlined some of the absurd fallacies of foreign aid: namely, if we give foreign aid at all, we must provide enough so that every foreign government in the world will always be able to get all it wants. We can exercise no choice in whom we give or lend our money to. If we give only "to the select few" we offend all others.

Congressman H. R. Gross (Republican, Iowa) asked a question:

"What interest rate will be charged upon the loans that are to be made?"

Congressman Carnahan:

"The legislation does not designate the interest rate."

Mr. Gross:

"What will be the length of the loan to be made?"

Mr. Carnahan:

"The legislation does not designate the length of the loans. The rules for the loans, which will determine the interest rates, the length of time the loans will run, the size of the installment repayments, and other administrative details, will be taken care of by the Executive Department."

Congressman John L. Pilcher (Democrat, Georgia) made the point that the manager of the Development Loan Fund, appointed by the President, could lend money to:

"any foreign government or foreign government agency, to any corporation, any individual or any group of persons."

Congressman Carnahan:

"That is correct."

Congressman Pilcher:

"In other words, it would be possible for an individual to borrow $1 million or $5 million to set up some business in some foreign country, if the manager so agreed; is that correct?"

Congressman Carnahan:

"If they met the criteria set up for loans."

Congressman Pilcher:

"The manager . . . has the authority to collect or compromise any obligation in this fund. In other words, he can make a loan this month and if he so desires he can turn around and compromise it or cancel it next month which is a straight out grant in the disguise of a soft-loan program."

Congressman Porter Hardy, Jr. (Democrat, Virginia) said:

"The manager of the Fund has almost unlimited authority to do anything he pleases."

Congressman Barratt O'Hara (Democrat, Illinois), trying to quiet fears that this bill was granting unlimited, uncontrollable power to some appointed manager, said that the blank-check grant of authority was not really being made to the fund manager at all. The power was being given to the President of the United States, and the manager would merely "perform such functions with respect to this title as the President may direct."

Congressman Gross said:

"That is more power than any President should ask for or want the responsibility for."

Congressman Leon H. Gavin (Republican, Pennsylvania) pointed out that we already have 5 or 6 lending agencies in this field: The International Co-operation Administration; the Export-Import Bank; the International Bank; the International Monetary Fund; the International Development Corporation; and the World Bank. Why, then, do we need this new one, the Development Loan Fund?

Congressman Walter H. Judd (Republican, Minnesota) had already answered that question, explaining that Development Loan Fund money would go to foreigners who could not qualify for loans from other agencies.

Congressman Gross said that all foreign nations which will borrow from this Fund could get all the American private capital they need if they had political systems which made lending to them sensible or feasible.

In short, the Development Loan Fund (which the Committee for Economic Development boasts paternity of) is a scheme for giving American tax money to foreigners who have proven themselves such poor credit risks that they cannot obtain loans even from other governmental and UN agencies–and who will use the money to line their own pockets and to build socialistic enterprises which will eliminate possibilities of freedom in their own land, and will compete in world markets with American enterprise.

* * * * *

In its 1957 annual report, the CED also boasted about the work of its Area Development Committee. At that time, the two leading members of this particular committee of the CED (who were also members of the Council on Foreign Relations) were Mr. Stanley Marcus, President of Neiman-Marcus Co., in Dallas; and the late Dr. Beardsley Ruml, widely known New Deal socialist "economist." Mr. Jervis J. Babb, Chairman of the CED's Area Development Committee (President of Lever Brothers Company) said:

> "The new area development program, approved by the Trustees [of CED] at their May [1957] meeting in Chicago is underway ... Already, close relationships have been established with organizations, both public and private, that are conducting research and administering programs relating to area development ...
>
> "Five of CED's College-Community Research Centers ... have been selected as a starting point of CED's area development pilot projects. The five centers are: Boston, Utica, Alabama, Arkansas, and Oklahoma."

The CED's Area Development work has brought CED personnel into close cooperation with the collection of tax-exempt "municipal planning" organizations housed in a Rockefeller-financed center at 1313 East 60th Street, Chicago, which has become national headquarters for the production and placement of experts–who fabricate "progressive" legislation for government at all levels; who rewrite our "archaic" state constitutions; and who take over as city managers, or county managers, or metropolitan managers, or regional managers whenever people in any locality have progressed to the point of accepting government by imported experts as a substitute for government by elected local citizens.

In other words, through the Area Development activities of the Committee for Economic Development, the invisible government of America–the Council on Foreign Relations–has a hand in the powerful drive for Metropolitan Government. Metropolitan Government, as conceived by socialist planners, would destroy the whole fabric of government and social organization in the United States.

* * * * *

Metropolitan Government would eliminate the individual states as meaningful political entities, would divide the nation into metropolitan regions sprawling across state lines, and would place the management of these regional governments in the hands of appointed experts answerable not to local citizens but to the supreme political power in Washington. (For detailed discussion, see The Dan Smoot Report, April 13 and 20, 1959, "Metropolitan Government–Part One," and "Metropolitan Government–Part Two.")

Through the Area Development activities of the Committee for Economic Development, the Council on Foreign Relations has supported the Urban Renewal program.

Urban Renewal with federal tax money was authorized in the National Housing Act of 1949, and enlarged in scope by amendments to the Housing Acts of 1954, 1956, and 1957; but it did not become a vigorously promoted nationwide program until late 1957, after the Council on Foreign Relations (through the CED) started pushing it.

* * * * *

Urban Renewal is a federally financed program of city planning which requires city governments to seize homes and other private property from some citizens and re-sell them, at below cost, to real estate promoters and other private citizens for developments that the city planners consider desirable.

Under the ancient, but awesome, right of eminent domain, city governments do not have the power to take private real estate from one citizen for the profit of another citizen. But in November, 1954, the

Supreme Court in an urban renewal case, said that Congress and state legislature can do anything they like to the private property of private citizens as long as they claim they are doing it for public good.

Federal urban renewal has opened rich veins of public money for graft, corruption, and political vote buying; and it is destroying private property rights under the pretext that clearing slums will eliminate the causes of crime. Moreover, urban renewal authorizes the seizure not just of slum property, but of all private property in a whole section of a city, for resale to private interests which promise to build something that governmental planners will like.

Federal urban renewal–since the Council on Foreign Relation's CED started supporting it–has become a national movement with frightful implications and dangers. (For detailed discussion of urban renewal, see The Dan Smoot Report, September 29, 1958, and October 6, 1958.)

* * * * *

In its 1957 Annual Report, the Committee for Economic Development gave details on its educational work in public schools and colleges. This work was, at that time, carried on primarily by the CED's Business-Education Committee, and by two subsidiary operations which that Committee created: the College-Community Research Centers and the Joint Council on Economic Education. From the 1957 Annual Report of the Committee for Economic Development:

> "CED's efforts to promote and improve economic education in the schools are of special appeal to those who are concerned . . . both with education and the progress of the free enterprise system. The Business-Education program and the numerous College-Community Research Centers it has sponsored, together with the use of CED publications as teaching materials,

represent an important contribution to economic education on the college level.

"In the primary and secondary schools, the introduction of economics into teaching programs is moving forward steadily, thanks largely to the Joint Council on Economic Education which CED helped to establish and continues to support . . .

"The Business-Education Committee continued in 1957 its work with the College-Community Research Centers and with the Joint Council on Economic Education.

"The Joint Council's program to improve the teaching of economics in the public schools is now operating in 39 states, and the 25 college-community research centers active last year brought to more than 3000 the number of business and academic men who have worked together on economic research projects of local and regional importance . . .

"In its work, the committee [Business-Education Committee] is finding especially valuable the experience gained through the operation of the College-Community Research Centers. These centers are financed partly by CED, partly by the Fund for Adult Education [a Ford Foundation operation] and partly by locally-raised funds . . .

"The Joint Council [on Economic Education] is making excellent progress in training teachers and incorporating economics education in all grade levels of public school systems. In addition to its national service programs, the Council has developed strong local or state councils which not only help guide its work but last year raised more than $500,000 to finance local projects.

"CED helped to establish and works closely with this independent organization [Joint Council on Economic Education] which is now conducting four major types of activities.

"1. Summer Workshops for Teachers. These working sessions, sponsored by colleges and universities, provide three weeks training in economics and develop ways to incorporate economics into the school curriculum. Over 19,000 persons have participated since the program began.

"2. Cooperating School Program. Twenty school systems are working with the Joint Council [on Economic Education] to demonstrate how economics can be incorporated into the present curriculum . . .

"3. College Program. Few students majoring in education now take economics courses; therefore, 20 leading institutions are working with the Joint Council [on Economic Education] to develop better training in economics for prospective teachers . . .

"4. High School-Community Projects. The Joint Council [on Economic Education] is helping to conduct demonstration programs which show how students can use community resources to improve their economics education. For example, the Whittier, California school system conducted a six-week program to help high school seniors understand the kind of economy in which they would live and work. They joined in research studies on regional economic problems being carried on by the Southern California College-Community research center . . ."

The Committee for Economic Development claims that its educational work in economics is dedicated to progress of free enterprise; and many of its programs in schools and colleges are educational; but its subtle and relentless emphasis is on the governmental interventionism that is the essence of New-Dealism, Fair-Dealism, Modern-Republicanism, and New-Frontierism—the governmental interventionism prescribed long ago as the way to socialize the economy of America in preparation for integrating this nation into a worldwide socialist system.

* * * * *

Paul Hoffman's CED has come a long way since 1942. In 1957, the CED's College-Community Research Centers had "Projects in Progress" in 33 institutions of higher learning:

Bates College, Boston College, Boston University, Bowdoin College, Brown University, Colby College, Dartmouth College, Emory University, Harvard Graduate School of Business Administration, Iowa State College, Lewis & Clark College, McGill University, Northeastern University, Northwestern University, Occidental College, Pomona College, Reed College, Rutgers University, Southern Methodist University, Tulane University, University of Alabama, University of Arkansas, University of Iowa, University of Maine, University of Michigan, University of Minnesota, University of North Carolina, University of Oklahoma, University of Pennsylvania, University of Washington, University of Wisconsin, Utica College of Syracuse University, and Washington University.

* * * * *

In 1957, the following institutions of higher learning were participating in the CED's Joint Council on Economic Education "College Program" to develop training in economics for prospective teachers:

Brigham Young University, George Peabody College for Teachers, Indiana University, Montclair State Teachers College, New York University, Ohio State University, Oklahoma A & M College, Pennsylvania State University, Purdue University,

Syracuse University, Teachers College of Columbia University, University of Colorado, University of Connecticut, University of Illinois, University of Iowa, University of Minnesota, University of Southern California, University of Tennessee, University of Texas, University of Washington.

* * * * *

In 1957, the following 20 school systems were working in the CED's Joint Council on Economic Education "Cooperating School Program," to demonstrate how economics can be incorporated in the school curriculum, beginning in the first grade:

Akron, Ohio; Albion, Illinois; Chattanooga, Tennessee; Colton, California; Dayton, Ohio; Fort Dodge, Iowa; Hartford, Connecticut; Kalamazoo, Michigan; Lexington, Alabama; Minneapolis, Minnesota; New York City, New York; Portland, Oregon; Providence, Rhode Island; Ridgewood, New Jersey; Seattle, Washington; Syracuse, New York; University City, Missouri; Webster Groves, Missouri; West Hartford, Connecticut; Whittier, California.

As indicated, the Business-Education Committee of the CED is the select group which supervises this vast "educational" effort reaching into public schools, colleges, and communities throughout the nation:

James L. Allen, Senior Partner of Booz, Allen & Hamilton; Jervis J. Babb, Chairman of the Board of Lever Brothers, Company; Sarah G. Blanding, President of Vassar College; W. Harold Brenton, President of Brenton Brothers, Inc.; James F. Brownlee, former government official who is Chairman of the Board of the Minute Maid Corporation, and a director of many other large corporations, such as American Sugar Refining Co., Bank of Manhattan, Gillette Safety Razor, R. H. Macy Co., Pillsbury Mills, American Express; Everett Needham Case, President of Colgate University; James B. Conant, former President of Harvard and Ambassador to Germany; John T. Connor, President of Merck & Co.; John S. Dickey, President of Dartmouth College; John M. Fox, President of Minute Maid Corporation; Paul S. Gerot, President of Pillsbury Mills; Stanley Marcus, President of Neiman-Marcus; W. A. Patterson, President of United Air Lines; Morris B. Pendleton, President of Pendleton Tool Industries; Walter Rothschild, Chairman of the Board of Abraham & Straus; Thomas J. Watson, Jr., President of International Business Machines Corporation; J. Cameron Thomson, Chairman of the Board of Northwest Bancorporation.

Note that three of these CED Business-Education Committee members–Conant, Dickey, and Marcus–are influential members of the Council on Foreign Relations and have many connections with the big foundations financing the great CFR interlock.

* * * * *

In addition to the educational work which it discusses in its 1957 Annual Report, the Committee for Economic Development utilizes many other means to inject its (and the CFR's) economic philosophies into community thought-streams throughout the nation.

Here, for example, are passages from a news story in The Dallas Morning News, June 30, 1953:

"Dallas businessmen and Southern Methodist University officials Monday [June 29] launched a $25,000 business research project financed through agencies of the Ford Foundation.

"Stanley Marcus of Dallas, a national trustee of Ford Foundation's Committee for Economic Development, said the project would go on two or three years under foundation funds. After that . . . the City might foot the bill . . .

"The SMU project–along with several others like it throughout the nation–is designed to foster study in regional and local business problems, Marcus commented.

"Here's how the Dallas project will work:

"A business executive committee, composed of some of Dallas' top businessmen, will be selected. These men then will select a group of younger executives for a business executive research committee. This will be the working group, Marcus explained . . .

"At SMU, several of the schools' chief officials will act as a senior faculty committee . . . Acting as co-ordinator for the project will be Warren A. Law . . . who soon will get his doctorate in economics from Harvard University."

The "experimental" stage of this Business Executives Research Committee lasted five years in Dallas. During that time, the researchers filed two major reports: an innocuous one in 1955 concerning traffic and transit problems in Dallas; and a most significant one in 1956, strongly urging metropolitan government for Dallas County, patterned after the metro system in Toronto, Canada.

* * * * *

In October, 1958, Dr. Donald K. David, then Chairman of the Committee for Economic Development and Vice Chairman of the Ford Foundation (and also a member of the Council on Foreign Relations) went to Dallas to speak to the Citizens Council, an organization composed of leading Dallas business executives, whose president that year was Stanley Marcus.

92

Dr. David told the business men that they should give greater support and leadership to the government's foreign aid program; and, of course, he urged vast expansion of foreign aid, particularly to "underdeveloped nations."

That was the signal and the build-up. The next month–November, 1958–the experimental Business Executives Research Committee, which the CED had formed in 1953 and which had already completed its mission with its report and recommendation on metropolitan government for Dallas, was converted into "The Dallas CED Associates."

Here is a news story about that event, taken from the November 11, 1958, Dallas Morning News:

"A Dallas Committee for Economic Development–the first of its kind in the nation–has been founded at Southern Methodist University. It will give voice to Southwestern opinions–and knowledge–on economic, matters or international importance. Keystone will be an economic research center to be established soon at SMU.

"A steering group composed of Dallas and Southwestern business, industrial and educational leaders laid the groundwork for both committee and center in a weekend meeting at SMU."

The "steering group" included George McGhee and Neil Mallon.

Mr. McGhee (presently Assistant Secretary of State for Policy Planning) is, and has been for many years, a member of the Council on Foreign Relations.

Neil Mallon, then Chairman of the Board of Dresser Industries and a former official of the Foreign Policy Association, founded the Dallas Council on World Affairs in 1951. Dresser Industries is one of the big corporations which contribute money to the Council on Foreign Relations.

93

In the group with Mr. McGhee and Mr. Mallon were five SMU officials, a Dallas banker, a real estate man, and Stanley Marcus, the head man in the "steering group" which set up the Dallas Associates of the Committee for Economic Development.

The first literary product of the Dallas Associates of the CED—at least, the first to come to my attention—is a most expensive-looking 14-page printed booklet entitled "The Role of Private Enterprise in the Economic Development of Underdeveloped Nations." The title page reveals that this pamphlet is a policy statement of The Dallas Associates of CED. It is little more than a rewrite of the speech which Dr. Donald K. David had made to the Dallas Citizens Council in November, 1958, urging business to give support and leadership to the government's foreign aid programs.

CHAPTER 5.

BUSINESS ADVISORY COUNCIL

Whereas the Foreign Policy Association-World Affairs Center is primarily interested in fostering the foreign policy desired by the CFR, and the Committee for Economic Development is primarily interested in formulating economic and other policies which, through governmental controls, will lead us into total socialism–another, smaller (but, in some ways, more powerful) organization has (or, until mid-1961, had) the primary responsibility of infiltrating government: of selecting men whom the CFR wants in particular jobs, and of formulating, inside the agencies of government, policies which the CFR wants. This small but mighty organization was the Business Advisory Council.

Daniel C. Roper, F. D. Roosevelt's Secretary of Commerce, formed the Business Advisory Council on June 26, 1933. Roper set it up as a panel of big businessmen to act as unofficial advisers to President Roosevelt. He was disappointed in it, however. The biggest businessmen in America did, indeed, join; but they did not support the total New Deal as Roper had expected they would when he made them "advisers."

Roper, however, was a figurehead. The brains behind the formation of the Business Advisory Council were in the head of Sidney J. Weinberg, Senior Partner of the New York investment house of Goldman, Sachs & Co.–and also on the boards of directors of about thirty of the biggest corporations in America. Weinberg helped organize the BAC. He recruited most of its key members. He was content to let America's big businessmen ripen for a while in the sunshine of the New Deal's "new" philosophy of government, before expecting them to give that philosophy full support.

Secretary of Commerce Daniel C. Roper pouted and ignored the Business Advisory Council when he discovered that the big businessmen, enrolled as governmental "advisors," tried to advise things that governmental leaders did not like. But Sidney Weinberg was shrewd, and had a definite, long-range plan for the Business Advisory Council. He held the BAC together as a kind of social club, keeping the big business men under constant exposure to the "new" economic philosophies of the New Deal, waiting for the propitious moment to enlist America's leading capitalists on the side of the socialist revolutionaries, determined to destroy capitalism and create a one-world socialist society.

* * * * *

The right time came in 1939, when World War II started in Europe and Roosevelt developed his incurable ambition to get in that war and become President of the World. Plans for America's frenzied spending on national defense began in 1939. With mammoth government contracts in the offing, Weinberg had no trouble converting the Business Advisory Council of leading businessmen into an agency for helping governmental leaders plan the policies for war and for the post-war period.

* * * * *

In September, 1960, Harper's Magazine published an article by Hobart Rowen, entitled "America's Most Powerful Private Club," with a sub-title, "How a semi-social organization of the very biggest businessmen–discreetly shielded from public scrutiny–is 'advising' the government on its top policy decisions." Here are passages from the article:

"The Business Advisory Council meets regularly with government officials six times a year . . . On two of these six occasions . . . the BAC convenes its sessions at plush resorts, and with a half-dozen or more important Washington officials and their wives as its guests, it indulges in a three-day 'work and play' meeting . . .

"The guest list is always impressive: on occasion, there have been more Cabinet officers at a . . . BAC meeting than were left in the Capital . . .

"These meetings cost the BAC anywhere from $6,000 to $12,000 or more, paid out of the dues of members . . . which have been judged tax-deductible by the Internal Revenue Service . . .

"After the 1952 election, the BAC was having its fall 'work and play' meeting at the Cloister, just off the Georgia coast and a short distance from Augusta, where Ike was alternating golf with planning his first-term Cabinet. [Sidney] Weinberg and [General Lucius D.] Clay [members of the BAC executive committee] . . . hustled . . . to Augusta, conferred with Ike [a 'close, intimate, personal friend' of both men] . . .

"The result was historic: Ike tapped three of the BAC leaders . . . for his Cabinet. They were Charles E. Wilson of General Motors as Defense Secretary; [George M.] Humphrey, then boss of the M. A. Hanna Co., as Treasury Secretary; and Robert T. Stevens of the J. P. Stevens & Co., as Army Secretary . . .

"Afterwards, [Secretary] Humphrey himself dipped into the BAC pool for Marion Folsom of Eastman Kodak as Under Secretary of the Treasury [later Secretary of Health, Education, and Welfare] . . .

"Membership in the Council gives a select few the chance to bring their views to bear on key government people, in a most pleasant, convivial, and private atmosphere . . .

"The BAC, powerful in its composition and with an inside track, is thus a special force. An intimation of its influence can be gleaned from its role in the McCarthy case . . . BAC helped push Senator Joe McCarthy over the brink in 1954, by supplying a bit of backbone to the Eisenhower Administration at the right time. McCarthy's chief target in the Army-McCarthy hearings was the aforementioned Robert T. Stevens—a big wheel in the BAC who had become Secretary of the Army. The BAC didn't pay much—if any—attention to Joe McCarthy as a social menace until he started to pick on Bob Stevens. Then, they burned up.

"During the May 1954 meeting at the Homestead [expensive resort hotel in Hot Springs, Virginia, where the BAC often holds its 'work and play' sessions with high government officials and their wives], Stevens flew down from Washington for a weekend reprieve from his televised torture. A special delegation of BAC officials made it a point to journey from the hotel to the mountaintop airport to greet Stevens. He was escorted into the lobby like a conquering hero. Then, publicly, one member of the BAC after another roasted the Eisenhower Administration for its McCarthy-appeasement policy. The BAC's attitude gave the Administration some courage, and shortly thereafter former Senator Ralph Flanders (a Republican and BAC member) introduced a Senate resolution calling for censure."

* * * * *

Active membership in the Business Advisory Council is limited to about 70. After a few years as an "active," a member can become a "graduate," still retaining his full voting and membership privileges.

I have obtained the names of 120 "active" and "graduate" members of the BAC, listed below. Those who are members of the Council on Foreign Relations are identified by "CFR" after their names.

Winthrop W. Aldrich (CFR)

William M. Allen (President of Boeing Airplane Company; member Board of Directors of Pacific National Bank of Seattle)

S. C. Allyn (CFR)

Robert B. Anderson

Clarence Avildsen (Chairman, Avildsen Tools & Machines, Inc.)

William M. Batten (President, J. C. Penney Company)

S. D. Bechtel (CFR)

S. Clark Beise (President, Bank of America; member Board of Directors, National Trust and Savings Association, San Francisco)

Roger M. Blough (CFR)

Harold Boeschenstein (President, Owens-Corning Fiberglas Corporation; Chairman of the Board, Fiberglas Canada, Ltd.; member of the Board of Directors of National Distillers Products Corporation, International Paper Company, Toledo Trust Company, Dow, Jones & Co.)

Fred Bohen (President of Meredith Publishing Company– Better Homes and Gardens, Better Farming; member of Board of Directors of Meredith Radio & Television Stations, Iowa, Northwest Bancorporation, Central Life Assurance Society, Allis-Chalmers Manufacturing Co., Northwestern Bell Telephone Co., Iowa-Des Moines National Bank)

Ernest R. Breech (Executive Vice President, Ford Motor, Company; member of Board of Directors of Transcontinental & Western Air, Inc., Pan-American Airways; President of Western Air Express)

George R. Brown (Chairman of the Board, Texas Eastern Transmission Corp.; Executive Vice President, Brown & Root, Inc. of Houston; President of Board of Trustees, Rice University)

Carter L. Burgess (CFR)

Paul C. Cabot (President of State Street Investment Corp.; partner in State Street Research & Management Co.; member of the Board of Directors of J. P. Morgan & Co., Continental Can Co., Inc., National Dairy Products Corp., Tampa Electric Co., The B. F. Goodrich Co.; Treasurer of Harvard University)

James V. Carmichael (President, Scripto, Inc.; member of Board of Directors of Lockheed Aircraft Corp., Trust Company of Georgia, Atlanta Transit Co., The Southern Co.)

Walker L. Cisler (CFR)

General Lucius D. Clay (CFR)

Will L. Clayton (CFR)

John L. Collyer (CFR)

Ralph J. Cordiner (Chairman of the Board and President of General Electric Co.)

John E. Corette (President of Montana Power Co.)

John Cowles (CFR)

C. R. Cox (CFR)

Harlow H. Curtice (retired President of General Motors Corp.; Chairman of the Board of Directors of Genesee Merchants Bank & Trust Co.; member of the Board of Directors of the National Bank of Detroit)

Charles E. Daniel (head of Daniel Construction Co., member of Board of Directors of First National Bank of Greenville, South Carolina, La France Industries, J. P. Stevens Co., Inc., Textron, Inc.; Trustee of Clemson College)

Donald K. David (CFR)

Paul M. Davies (President and Chairman of the Board of Food Machinery & Chemical Corp.; member of Board of Directors of American Trust Company of California, National Distillers Products Corp., Caterpillar Tractor Co.; Professor at Stanford University; Director of Stanford Research Institute, San Jose State

College, Pacific School of Religion; Trustee of Committee for Economic Development)

Frank R. Denton (Vice Chairman and Director of Mellon National Bank and Trust Company, Pittsburgh; member of the Board of Directors of Swindell-Dressler Corp., Westinghouse Electric Co., Jones & Laughlin Steel Corporation, Pullman, Inc., National Union Fire Insurance Co., Shamrock Oil & Gas Corp., M. W. Kellogg Co., Pullman Standard Car Manufacturing Co., Trailmobile, Inc., National Union Indemnity Co.; Trustee of Pennsylvania State University, Kansas University Endowment Association)

Charles D. Dickey (Vice President, member of the Board of Directors, and Chairman of the Executive Committee of Morgan Guaranty Trust Co.; member of the Board of Directors of General Electric Co., Beaver Coal, Kennekott Copper Corp., Braden Copper Co., Merck & Co., Inc., Panhandle Eastern Pipeline Co., New York Life Insurance Co., Church Life Insurance Corp., Church Fire Insurance Corp.)

Frederick G. Donner (CFR)

William Y. Elliott (CFR)

Ralph E. Flanders (CFR)

Marion B. Folsom (CFR)

Henry Ford II (President of Ford Motor Co.; Chairman of the Board of American Heritage Foundation)

William C. Foster (CFR)

G. Keith Funston (President of New York Stock Exchange; member of the Board of Directors of Metropolitan Life Insurance Co.; Trustee of Trinity College of Connecticut, Virginia Theological Seminary, Samuel H. Kress Foundation)

Frederick V. Geier (CFR)

Elisha Gray II (President and Director of Whirlpool Corp.)

Crawford H. Greenewalt (President and Director of E. I. du Pont de Nemours Company, Christiana Securities Company; member of the Board of Directors of Massachusetts Institute of Technology; Trustee of the Carnegie Institute, Washington)

General Alfred M. Gruenther (CFR)

Joseph B. Hall (President of Kroger Company, Manufacturers and Merchants Indemnity Co., Selective Insurance Co.; member of the Board of Directors of Robert A. Cline, Inc., AVCO Manufacturing Corp., Cincinnati and Suburban Bell Telephone Co., General Stores Corp.; member of the Board of the Federal Reserve Bank of Cleveland)

W. Averill Harriman (CPR)

William A. Hewitt (President and member of the Board of Directors of Deere & Company)

Milton P. Higgins (CFR)

Paul G. Hoffman (CFR)

Eugene Holman (CFR)

John Holmes (President, member of the Board of Directors, and retired Chairman of Swift & Company; member of the Board of Directors of Continental Illinois National Bank and Trust Company, General Electric Corporation)

Herbert Hoover, Jr. (CFR)

Preston Hotchkis (Vice Chairman of the Board of Directors and Treasurer of Founders' Insurance Company; Executive Vice President and member of the Board of Directors of Fred H. Bixby Ranch Company; member of the Board of Directors of Metropolitan Coach Lines, Pacific Mutual Life Insurance Co., Pacific Telephone & Telegraph Co., Blue Diamond Corp.)

Amory Houghton (CFR)

Theodore V. Houser (retired Chairman of the Board of Sears, Roebuck & Co.; member of the Board of Directors of Sears, Roebuck & Co., Bell and Howell Co., Quaker Oats Co.,

Barry L. Leithead (President and Director of Cluett, Peabody and Company, Inc.; Chairman of Cluett, Peabody and Company of Canada, Ltd.; member of the Board of Directors of B. F. Goodrich Company)

Augustus C. Long (Chairman of the Board of Texaco, Inc.; member of the Board of Directors of Freeport Sulphur Co., Equitable Life Assurance Society of the United States, Federal Reserve Bank of New York)

Donold B. Lourie (President and Director of Quaker Oats Company; member of the Board of Directors of Northern Trust Co., International Paper Co., Pure Oil Co.; Trustee of Princeton University)

George H. Love (Chairman of the Board of Pittsburgh-Consolidation Coal Company, M. A. Hanna Company; member of the Board of Directors of Union Carbide & Carbon Corp., Mellon National Bank & Trust Company of Pittsburgh, Pullman Co., General Electric Co., National Steel Corp., Hanna Mining Co.; Trustee of Princeton University, University of Pittsburgh)

James Spencer Love (Chairman of the Board of Burlington Mills Corp.; Chairman and President of Burlington Industries, Inc.; Trustee of University of North Carolina, Davidson College)

George P. MacNichol, Jr. (President and Director of Libbey-Owens-Ford Glass Company; member of the Board of Directors of Wyandotte Chemical Co., Federal Reserve Bank of Cleveland)

Roswell F. Magill (member of Cravath, Swaine & Moore, Lawyers; Trustee of Mutual Life Insurance Company of New York, Macy Foundation, Guggenheim Foundation)

Deane W. Malott (President, Cornell University; member of the Board of Directors of Pitney-Bowes, Inc., B. F. Goodrich Co., General Mills, Inc., Owens-Corning Fiberglas Corp.; former Vice President of Hawaiian Pineapple Co.; Professor of Business at Harvard, Chancellor of University of Kansas)

James W. McAfee (President of Union Electric Company of Missouri, Edison Electric Institute; member of the Board of Directors of St. Louis Union Trust Co., American Central Insurance Co., North American Co.)

S. Maurice McAshan (President, Anderson, Clayton & Company)

Thomas B. McCabe (CFR)

John L. McCaffrey (retired Chairman of International Harvester Co.; member of the Board of Directors of Harris Trust & Savings Bank of Chicago, American Telephone & Telegraph Co., Corn Products Co., Midwest Stock Exchange; Trustee of the University of Chicago, University of Notre Dame, Eisenhower Exchange Fellowships, Inc.)

Leonard F. McCollum (CFR)

Charles P. McCormick (Chairman of the Board and retired President of McCormick & Co., Inc.; member of the Board of Directors of Massachusetts Mutual Life Insurance Co., Equitable Trust Co. of Baltimore, Advertising Council; Chairman of the Board of Regents, University of Maryland)

Neil H. McElroy (Chairman of the Board, Procter & Gamble Co.; Secretary of Defense 1957-1961)

Earl M. McGowin (Vice President of W. T. Smith Lumber Co.; member of the Board of Directors of The Southern Company of New York, Alabama Power Co.)

James H. McGraw, Jr. (CFR)

Paul B. McKee (Chairman of Pacific Power & Light Co.)

John P. McWilliams (retired President and Chairman of the Board of Youngstown Steel Door Co.; member of the Board of Directors of National City Bank of Cleveland, Eaton Manufacturing Co., Goodyear Tire & Rubber Co., Union Carbide & Carbon Corp.)

105

George G. Montgomery (Chairman of Kern County Land Co.; member of the Board of Directors of American Trust Co., Bankers Trust Co., Castle & Cook, Ltd., General Electric Co., Matson Navigation Co., Matson Assurance Co., Oceanic Steam Ship Co., Pacific Lumber Co.)

Charles G. Mortimer (Chairman and retired President of General Foods Corp.; member of the Board of Directors of National City Bank of New York, Union Theological Seminary)

William B. Murphy (President of Campbell Soup Co.; member of the Board of Directors of Merck & Co.)

Aksel Nielsen (President of Title Guaranty Co., Mortgage Investments Co.; member of the Board of Directors of C. A. Norgren Co., United American Life Insurance Co., Landon Abstract Co., Empire Savings & Loan Association, United Airlines)

Thomas F. Patton (President and Director of Republic Steel Corp., Union Drawn Steel Co.; member of the Board of Directors of Air-Vue Products Corp., Maria Luisa Ore Co., Berger Manufacturing Company of Massachusetts, Iron Ore Company of Canada, Liberia Mining Co., Ltd., Liberian Navigation Corp., Union Commerce Bank, Tankore Corp., Standard Oil Company of Ohio; Trustee of Ohio State University)

Charles H. Percy (President and Director of Bell & Howell Co.; member of the Board of Directors of Chase Manhattan Bank, Harris Trust & Savings Bank, Burroughs Corp., Fund for Adult Education of the Ford Foundation; Trustee, University of Chicago)

Theodore S. Petersen (President and Director of Standard Oil of California; member of the Board of Directors of Pacific Mutual Insurance Co.; Trustee of Committee on Economic Development; consulting Professor, Stanford University)

Gwilym A. Price (Chairman and President of Westinghouse Electric Corp.; member of the Board of Directors of Mellon National Bank & Trust Company of Pittsburgh, Eastman-Kodak Co., Carnegie Corp., National Union Fire Insurance Co., Great Atlantic & Pacific Tea Co.; Trustee of Allegheny College, The Hanover Bank, Carnegie Institute, Carnegie Institute of Technology; Chairman of the Board of Trustees, University of Pittsburgh; Chairman of Crusade for Freedom)

Edgar Monsanto Queeny (Chairman of the Board, Monsanto Chemical Co.; member of the Board of Directors of American Airlines, Union Electric Co. of Missouri, Chemstrand Corp., Sicedison S.P.A. of Italy, World Rehabilitation Fund; Trustee Herbert Hoover Foundation)

Clarence B. Randall (Chairman of the Board, Inland Steel Co.; member of the Board of Directors, Bell & Howell Co.; Trustee, University of Chicago)

Philip D. Reed (CFR)

Richard S. Reynolds, Jr. (President of Reynolds Metals Co.; Chairman of the Board of Robertshaw-Fulton Controls Co.; member of the Board of Directors of Manufacturers Trust Co., British Aluminum, Ltd., U. S. Foil Co., Central National Bank of Richmond)

Winfield W. Riefler (CFR)

William E. Robinson (Chairman of the Coca-Cola Co.; member of the Board of Directors of Manufacturers Trust Co.; Coca-Cola Export Co., Libbey-Owens-Ford Glass Co., Trustee of New York University; former Director and Publisher of New York Herald-Tribune)

Donald J. Russell (President and Director of Southern Pacific Co.; Texas and New Orleans Railroad Co.; Chairman of the Board of St. Louis-Southwestern Railroad; Director of Stanford Research Institute; Trustee of Stanford University)

Stuart T. Saunders (President of Norfolk and Western Railway; Director of First and Merchants National Bank of Richmond)

Blackwell Smith (CPR)

C. R. Smith (President, American Airlines)

Lloyd B. Smith (President, A. O. Smith Corp.; Chairman, A. O. Smith of Texas)

John W. Snyder (Executive Vice President, Overland Corp.; Secretary of Treasury of the United States 1946-1953)

Joseph P. Spang, Jr. (retired President and Chairman of Gillette Co.; member of the Board of Directors of Gillette Co., Sheraton Corp. of America, First National Bank of Boston, U. S. Steel Corp., International Packers, Ltd.)

A. E. Staley, Jr. (Chairman of A. E. Staley Manufacturing Co.; Trustee, Millikin University)

Frank Stanton (President, Columbia Broadcasting System; Chairman of Center for Advanced Study in Behavioral Sciences; Trustee of Rand Corp.; member of the Board of Directors of New York Life Insurance Co.)

Robert T. Stevens (President and former Chairman of the Board, J. P. Stevens & Co.; member of the Board of Directors of General Electric Co., Owens-Corning Fiberglas Corp.; Trustee of Mutual Life Insurance Co. of New York; Secretary of the Army 1953-1955)

Hardwick Stires (partner, Scudder, Stevens & Clark Investment Counsels)

Lewis L. Strauss (CFR)

H. Gardiner Symonds (Chairman and President of Tennessee Gas and Transmission Company of Houston; Vice Chairman of Petro-Texas Chemical Corp.; Chairman of Bay Petroleum Corp., Tennessee-Venezuela South America, Chaco Petroleum of South America, Tennessee de Ecuador, South America, Tennessee-Argentina, Midwest Gas Transmission Co.; member of the Board

Inc., Continental Can Co., Inc., General Cigar Co., General Electric Co., General Foods Corp., B. F. Goodrich Co., Ford Motor Co., McKesson & Robbins, Inc., National Dairy Products Corp., Champion Paper & Fibre Co., Van Raalte Co., Inc.; former Governor of New York Stock Exchange)

    Walter H. Wheeler, Jr. (CFR)
    John Hay Whitney (CFR)
    Langbourne M. Williams (CFR)
    Thomas J. Watson, Jr. (CFR)

Of these 120 BAC members, 41 are members of the Council on Foreign Relations. Most of those who are not CFR members have affiliations with foundations or other organizations that are interlocked with the CFR.

Sidney Weinberg, for example (father of the BAC), is not listed (in any Council on Foreign Relations Annual Report in my files) as a member of the CFR; but he is a member of the board of many corporations which support the CFR; and has many close connections with CFR leaders through foundations and other CFR subsidiary agencies.

All Secretaries of Commerce since 1933 have served as ex-officio General Chairman of the BAC.

On July 10, 1961, Roger M. Blough announced that the Business Advisory Council had changed its name to Business Council; had severed its connection with the Commerce Department; and would in the future give its consultative services to any governmental agency that asked for them. The BAC had been under intense criticism for the expensive entertainment it had been giving to governmental officials it advised.

CHAPTER 6.

ADVERTISING COUNCIL

The Advertising Council, 25 West 45th Street, New York 36, N. Y. (with offices at 203 North Wabash Avenue, Chicago; 1200 18th Street, N. W., Washington; 425 Bush Street, San Francisco) serves as a public relations operation to promote selected projects supported by the Council on Foreign Relations and its interlocking affiliates.

The Advertising Council was created in 1942 (then called War Advertising Council) as a tax-exempt, non-governmental agency to promote wartime programs of government: rationing, salvage, the selling of war bonds, and so on.

The Advertising Council's specific job was to effect close cooperation between governmental agencies and business firms using the media of mass communication. A governmental agency would bring a particular project (rationing, for example) to the Advertising Council, for help in "selling" the project to the public. The Council would enlist the aid of some advertising agency. The agency (giving its services for nothing, as a contribution to the war effort) would prepare signs, newspaper mats, advertising layouts, broadcasting kits and what not. The Advertising Council might then enlist the free services of a public relations firm to get this material into newspapers and magazines; get it inserted in the regular ads of business firms; get it broadcast, free, as public-service spot announcements by radio networks; get it inserted into regular commercials on radio broadcasts; get slogans and art work stamped on the envelopes and business forms of corporations.

The Advertising Council rendered a valuable service to advertisers, broadcasting organizations, and publishers. Everyone wanted to support projects that would help the war effort. The Advertising Council did the important job of screening—of presenting projects which were legitimate and urgent.

Even the advertising agencies and public relations firms, which contributed free services, profited from the arrangement. They earned experience and prestige as agencies which had prepared nationally successful campaigns.

* * * * *

The Advertising Council continued after the war to perform this same service—selecting, for free promotion, projects that are "importantly in the public interest." Indeed, the service is more valued in peace time than in war by many advertisers and broadcasting officials who are badgered to support countless causes and campaigns, most of which sound good but some of which may be objectionable. Investigating to screen the good from the bad is a major job. The Advertising Council does this job. The Council is respected by industry, by the public, and by government. It is safe to promote a project which the Advertising Council claims to be "importantly in the public interest."

Thus, officials of the Advertising Council have become czars in a most important field. They arbitrarily decide what is, and what is not, in the public interest. When the Advertising Council "accepts" a project, the most proficient experts in the world—leading Madison Avenue people—go to work, without charge, to create (and saturate the media of mass communication with) the skillful propaganda that "sells" the project to the public.

Officials of the Advertising Council are aware of their power as moulders of public opinion. Theodore S. Repplier, head of the Advertising Council, was quoted in a June, 1961, issue of Saturday Review, as saying:

"There are Washington officials hired to collect figures on about every known occupation, to worry about the oil and miners under the ground, the rain in the sky, the wildlife in the woods, and the fish in the streams—but it is nobody's job to worry about America's state of mind, or whether Americans misread a situation in a way that could be tragic.

"This is a dangerous vacuum. But it is also a vacuum which explains to a considerable degree the important position the Advertising Council holds in American life today."

Note, particularly, that the Advertising Council is responsible to no one. If a business firm should decide on its own to include some "public service" project in its advertising, and the project evoked public indignation, the business firm would lose customers. The Advertising Council has no customers to please. Yet, the Advertising Council is a private agency, beyond the reach of voter and taxpayer indignation which, theoretically, can exercise some control over public agencies.

* * * * *

Who are these autocrats who have become so powerful that they can condition, if not control, public opinion? They are the members of the Public Policy Committee of the Advertising Council. Here were the 19 members of the Advertising Council's Committee, on June 23, 1958:

Sarah Gibson Blanding, President of Vassar College; Ralph J. Bunche, United Nations Under Secretary; Benjamin J. Buttenwieser,

113

partner in Kuhn, Loeb & Co.; Olive Clapper, publicist; Evans Clark, member of the New York Times editorial board; Helen Hall, Director of Henry Street Settlement; Paul G. Hoffman, Chairman of this Public Policy Committee; Charles S. Jones, President of Richfield Oil Corporation; Lawrence A. Kimpton, Chancellor of University of Chicago; A. E. Lyon, Executive Secretary of the Railway Labor Executives Association; John J. McCloy, Chairman of the Chase Manhattan Bank; Eugene Meyer, Chairman of the Washington Post & Times-Herald; William I. Myers, Dean of Agriculture at Cornell University; Elmo Roper, public opinion analyst; Howard A. Rusk, New York University Bellevue Medical Center; Boris Shishkin, Assistant to the President of AFL-CIO; George N. Shuster, President of Hunter College; Thomas J. Watson, Jr., President of International Business Machines Corporation; Henry M. Wriston, Executive Director of the American Assembly.

Of these 19, 8 are members of the Council on Foreign Relations–Bunche, Buttenwieser, Hoffman, McCloy, Roper, Shishkin, Shuster, Wriston. The remaining 11 are mostly "second level" affiliates of the CFR, or under the thumb of CFR members in the business world.

* * * * *

Some Advertising Council projects really are "in the public interest." The "Stop Accidents" campaign and the "Smokey Bear" campaign to prevent forest fires are among several which probably have done much good.

There has never been an Advertising Council project which insinuated anything to remind anyone of the basic American political idea written into our organic documents of government–the idea that men are endowed by God with inalienable rights; that the greatest threat to those rights

114

is the government under which men live; and that government, while necessary to secure the God-given blessings of liberty, must be carefully limited in power by an inviolable Constitution. But there have been many Advertising Council projects which were vehicles for the propaganda of international socialism.

The Advertising Council has promoted Law Day, which is an annual occasion for inundating America with "World Peace Through World Law" propaganda, designed to prepare the people for giving the World Court jurisdiction over American affairs, as a major step toward world government (see The Dan Smoot Report, September 14, 1959, "The World Court").

The Advertising Council has promoted the "mental health" project, which, superficially, appears to be an admirable effort to make the public aware of the truth that we have more mentally ill people than we have facilities for–but whose underlying, and dubious, purpose is to promote the passage, in all states, of "mental health" laws fabricated by international socialists in the World Health Organization and in the U. S. Public Health Service. These laws, to "facilitate access to hospital care" for mentally ill people, provide no new facilities, prescribe no better treatment, nor do anything else to relieve the suffering of sick people.

The new "mental health" laws, which the Advertising Council is helping to persuade people in all states to accept, eliminate the constitutional safeguards of a person accused of being mentally ill, thus making it easier for bureaucrats, political enemies and selfish relatives to commit him and get him out of the way.

The Advertising Council has touted ACTION–American Council to Improve Our Neighborhoods, Box 462, Radio City Station, New York 20, N. Y.–an organization for urban renewal. Of the 66 persons on the ACTION Board of Directors, a controlling majority are:

known members of the Council on Foreign Relations–such as Philip L. Graham and Stanley Marcus;

115

known members of important CFR affiliates—such as, Sidney Weinberg of the Business Advisory Council;

union bosses like Harry C. Bates, Ben Fischer, Joseph D. Keenan, Jacob S. Potofsky, Walter Reuther;

bureaucrats in charge of various "Housing Authorities," including Dr. Robert Weaver, Kennedy's present Housing Administrator whose appointment was challenged in the Senate because of Dr. Weaver's alleged communist front record;

"liberal" politicians dedicated to the total socialist revolution—such as, Joseph S. Clark, Jr., U. S. Senator from Pennsylvania;

officials of construction and real estate firms which can make mammoth profits on urban renewal projects and who are also "liberal" in their support of all governmental controls and subsidies, the tools for converting capitalism into socialism—such as, William Zeckendorf;

representatives of organizations also "liberal" in the sense indicated above—such as, Philip M. Klutznick of B'nai B'rith, and Mrs. Kathryn H. Stone of the League of Women Voters.

* * * * *

The Advertising Council supports United Nations propaganda.

The 1959 annual report of the United States Committee for the United Nations pays special tribute to the "radio-TV campaign, conducted through the cooperation of the Advertising Council and the National Association of Broadcasters." Here are some passages, from this tribute, which show how the Advertising Council gets one-world socialist propaganda into millions of American homes:

"Perry Como read the UN spot personally to his audience of 33,000,000."

"Jack Paar . . . [showed] a filmed visit to the UN by his daughter, Randy . . . following a splendid statement [by Paar]. This 7-minute segment of the show reached a minimum of 30,000,000 viewers."

"The campaign received tremendous recognition also on Meet the Press, the Today Show, I Love Lucy, the Desilu Playhouse, and the Jack Benny Show, among many others."

"Broadcast kits went out to every radio and television station in the country."

A recent accomplishment of the Advertising Council was its saturation bombing (1961) of the American public with propaganda in support of Kennedy's Youth Peace Corps.

CHAPTER 7.

UNITED NATIONS AND WORLD GOVERNMENT PROPAGANDA

All American advocates of supra-national government, or world government, claim their principal motive is to achieve world peace. Yet, these are generally the same Americans whose eager interventionism helped push America into the two world wars of this century.

The propaganda for involving America in the bloodshed and hatreds of Europe–in World War I and World War II–was the same as that now being used to push us into world government. In World War I, we rushed our soldiers across the wide seas to die in the cause of making the world safe for democracy–of eliminating evil in the world so that there would not be any more war! This was precisely what the world-government interventionists wanted us to do. The so-called American isolationists were not pacifists who recommended refusal to take up arms in defense of their own country: most of them were patriots who would have been among the foremost to fight in defense of America. Being intelligent citizens of a peaceful and civilized nation, they wanted to keep it that way.

The world-government interventionists used the extraordinary arguments of a man who, though living in an orderly and law-abiding neighborhood, says that he must go carousing around in adjoining communities and get involved in every street fight and barroom brawl he can find in order to avoid violence! Such a man not only becomes a party to lawless violence which he claims to deplore, but also creates hatreds and resentments which will ultimately bring to the sane citizens of his own peaceful neighborhood the evils which they had managed to keep out.

This is what Woodrow Wilson's intervention in World War I did to the United States. It sacrificed the lives of 250,000 American men—not to mention the hundreds of thousands crippled and otherwise wrecked by war. But this sacrifice of American youth did not make the world safe for anything. It helped make the world a breeding place for communism, fascism, naziism, and other varieties of socialism; and it planted the seeds for a second world war more destructive than the first.

But the world-government interventionists—when their bloody crusade proved worse than a tragic failure—did not admit error. They tried to place all the blame on the isolationists who had tried to keep us from making the ghastly mistake.

* * * * *

If we had stayed out of World War I, the European powers would have arrived, as they have been doing for thousands of years, at some kind of negotiated peace which would have saved not only hundreds of thousands of American lives, but millions of European lives as well. By entering World War I, we merely converted it into total war, prolonged it, and made it more savage.

The destruction and slaughter of World War I created power vacuums and imbalances and economic chaos, which inevitably led to World War II.

Again, the world-government advocates, who claimed to want peace, insisted that we go to war. They also intensified their efforts to entangle America, irretrievably, in political and economic union with European nations so that there would never again be any possibility of the United States staying out of the endless wars and turmoil of the old world.

119

It is, perhaps, fruitless to question the motives of people leading the campaign to push America into world government. All organizations which have been active in this movement–World Fellowship, Inc., Federal Union, Inc., Atlantic Union Committee, United World Federalists, and so on–have had a sprinkling of communist-fronters among their directors and members. But they have also had the official support of many prominent and respected Americans: Harry Truman, Dwight Eisenhower, John Kennedy, Richard Nixon, Estes Kefauver, John Sparkman, Adlai Stevenson, Dean Acheson, John Foster Dulles, Christian Herter, cabinet officers; senators and congressmen; Supreme Court justices; prominent churchmen, businessmen, financiers, entertainers, judges, union officials; newspaper and magazine editors; famous columnists and radio-television commentators.

* * * * *

Although the cry of "peace" is the perennial clarion call of all world-government advocates, many of them have, in recent years, added the claim that their recommendations (for converting America into a province of world government) are means of "fighting communism." Indeed, some of the most vigorous advocates of one-worldism have wide reputations as anti-communists–Walter Judd, a Republican Congressman from Minnesota, for example. Even Clarence Streit (leader of the now-defunct Federal Union, Inc., and father of that organization's very active and influential tax-exempt successor, Atlantic Union Committee) has ugly things to say about communism.

The fact is that every step the United States takes toward political and economic entanglements with the rest of the world is a step toward realization of the end objective of communism: creating a one-world socialist political and economic system in which we will be one of the subjugated provinces.

Because of the wealth we have created as a free and independent nation, we would be the most heavily taxed province in any conceivable supra-national government—whether in a "limited, federal union of the western democracies," which is what the Atlantic Union Committee people say they want; or in a total one-world system, which is what all advocates of international union really have as their final goal.

Because of our population, however, we would have minority representation in any supra-national government now being planned.

Americans would be subjected to laws enacted by an international parliament in which we would have little influence; taxing us, regulating our economic activities, controlling our schools, and dictating our social and cultural relations with each other and with the rest of the world.

* * * * *

America was founded, populated, and developed by people seeking escape from oppressive governments in Europe. Now our own leaders ask us to give up the freedom and independence which our forebears won for us with blood and toil and valorous devotion to high ideals, to become subjects in a governmental system that would inevitably be more tyrannical than any which our forefathers rebelled against or any that presently exist. If the world government included the despotic and oligarchic and militaristic, and feudalistic and primitive systems of Asia, the Middle East, Africa, and Latin America, it would necessarily become the bloodiest and most oppressive tyranny the world has ever known.

Nowadays, when two or more nations amalgamate their economic, political, and social systems they necessarily take the lowest common denominator of freedom rather than the highest. In fact, they must take something lower than the lowest: the union government will be more restrictive than the government of any of the nations which formed the union.

121

This will be true of any supra-national government that the United States might get into: the union will not extend American freedom to other nations; it will extend to all nations in the union the most restrictive controls of the most oppressive government which enters the union, and make even those controls worse than they were before the union was formed–because the American principle of federalism has been discarded by the "liberals" who manage our national affairs; and American federalism is the only political principle ever to exist in the history of the world that can make individual human freedom possible in a federation of states.

Hard core American communists know (and some admit) that any move toward American membership in any kind of supra-national government is a move toward the Soviet objective of a one-world socialist dictatorship; but all other American advocates of international union claim their schemes are intended to repeat and extend the marvelous achievement of 13 American states which, by forming a political union, created a free and powerful nation.

All United States advocates of any kind of world government point to the founding of America: 13 sovereign states, each one proud and nationalistic, all with special interests that were divergent from or in conflict with the interests of the others; yet, they managed to surrender enough sovereignty to join a federal union which gave the united strength of all, while retaining the individuality and freedom of each.

* * * * *

The 13 American states, in forming a federal union, did not take the lowest common denominator of freedom; they took the highest, and elevated that.

The American principle of federalism (indeed, the whole American constitutional system) grew out of the philosophical doctrine (or, rather, statement of faith) which Jefferson wrote into the Declaration of Independence:

> ". . . all men are . . . endowed by their Creator with certain inalienable rights . . ."

Men get their rights from God, not from government. Government, a man-made creature, has nothing except what it takes from God-created men. Government can give the people nothing that it has not first taken away from them. Hence, if man is to remain free, he must have a government which will play a very limited and negative role in his private affairs.

The United States is the only nation, ever, whose institutions and organic law were founded on this principle. The United Nations' Declaration of Human Rights; the Constitution of the Soviet Union; and the written and unwritten constitutions of every other nation in the world are all built on a political principle exactly opposite in meaning to the basic principle of Americanism. That is, the Constitution of the Soviet Union, and of every UN agency, and of all other nations, specify a large number of rights and privileges which citizens should have, if possible, and which government will grant them if government can, and if government thinks proper.

Contrast this with the American Constitution and Bill of Rights which do not contain one statement or inference that the federal government has any responsibility, or power, to grant the people rights, privileges, or benefits of any kind. The total emphasis in these American documents is on telling the federal government what it cannot do to and for the people—on ordering the federal government to stay out of the private affairs of citizens and to leave their God-given rights alone.

* * * * *

123

This negative, restricted role of the federal government, and this assumption that God and not government is the source of man's rights and privileges, are clearly stated in the Preamble to our Constitution. The Preamble says that this Constitution is being ordained and established, not to grant liberties to the people, but to secure the liberties which the people already had (before the government was ever formed) as blessings.

The essence of the American constitutional system, which made freedom in a federal union possible, is clearly stated in the first sentence of the first Article of our Constitution and in the last Article (the Tenth Amendment) of our Bill of Rights.

The first Article of our Constitution begins with the phrase, "All legislative Powers herein granted . . ." That obviously meant the federal government had no powers which were not granted to it by the Constitution. The Tenth Amendment restates the same thing with emphasis:

"The powers not delegated to the United States by the Constitution, nor prohibited by it to the States, are reserved to the States respectively, or to the people."

Clearly and emphatically, our Constitution says that the federal government cannot legally do anything which is not authorized by a specific grant of power in the Constitution.

This is the one constitutional concept that made the American governmental system different from all others; it is the one which left our people so free and unmolested by their own government that they converted the backward, American continent into the land of freedom, the most fruitful and powerful nation in history.

And this was the constitutional proviso which created the American principle of federalism. The Constitution made no grant, or even inferred a grant, of power to the federal government for meddling, to any extent, or for any purpose whatever, in the private cultural, economic, social, educational, religious, or political affairs of individual citizens–or in the legitimate governmental activities of the individual states which became members of the federal union. Hence, states could join the federal union without sacrificing the freedom of their citizens.

Modern "liberalism" which has been continuously in control of the federal government (and of most opinion-forming institutions and media throughout our society) since Franklin D. Roosevelt's first inauguration, March 4, 1933, has, by ignoring constitutional restraints, changed our Federal government with limited powers into a Central government with limitless power over the individual states and their people.

Modern "liberalism" has abandoned American constitutional government and replaced it with democratic centralism, which, in fundamental theory, is identical with the democratic centralism of the Soviet Union, and of every other major nation existing today.

It was possible to enlarge the size of the old American federal union without diminishing freedom for the people. When you enlarge the land area and population controlled by democratic centralism you must necessarily diminish freedom for the people, because the problems of centralized government increase with the size of population and area which it controls.

* * * * *

Look at what has happened to America since our federal government was converted into a centralized absolutism. The central government in Washington arrogated to itself the unconstitutional power and responsibility of regulating the relationships between private employers and their employees, enacting laws which established "collective bargaining" as "national policy," and which, to that end, gave international unions a virtual monopoly over large segments of the labor market.

It follows that a minor labor dispute between two unions on the waterfront of New York is no longer a concern only of the people and police in that neighborhood. A handful of union members who have no grievance whatever against their employers but who are in a jurisdictional struggle with another union, can shut down the greatest railroad systems in the world, throw thousands out of work, and paralyze vital transportation for business firms and millions of citizens all over the nation.

Harry Bridges on the West Coast can order a political demonstration having nothing to do with "labor" matters, and paralyze the economy of half the nation.

Imagine what it will be like if we join a world government. Then a dock strike in London will cripple, not just the British Isles but the whole world.

Now, the central government in Washington sends troops into local communities to enforce, at bayonet point, the illegal edicts of a Washington judicial oligarchy concerning the operation of local schools. If we join world government, the edict and the troops will come (depending on what nations are in the international union, of course) from India and Japan and the Congo.

* * * * *

There was a time when Americans, learning of suffering and want in a distant land, could respond to their Christian promptings and native kindliness by making voluntary contributions for relief to their fellow human beings abroad. Our central government's foreign aid programs have already taken much of that freedom away from American citizens—taxing them so heavily for what government wants to give away, that private citizens can't spend their own money the way they would like to.

What will it be like if we join a world government that embraces the real have-not nations of the earth? The impoverished subcontinent of India, because of population, would have more representatives in the international parliament than we would have. They, with the support of representatives from Latin America and Africa, could easily vote to lay a tax on "surplus" incomes for the benefit of all illiterate and hungry people everywhere; and outvoted Americans would be the only people in the world with incomes high enough to meet the international definition of "surplus."

We read with horror of Soviet slaughter in Hungary when the Soviets suppress a local rebellion against their partial world-government. What kind of horror would we feel after we join a world government and see troops from Europe and Africa and the Middle East machinegunning people on the streets of United States cities in order to suppress a rebellion of young Americans who somehow heard about the magnificent constitutional system and glorious freedom their fathers used to have and who are trying to make a public demonstration of protest against the international tyranny being imposed upon them?

A genuine world government might eliminate the armed conflict (between nations) which we now call war; but it would cause an endless series of bloody uprisings and bloody suppressions, and would cause more human misery than total war itself.

* * * * *

In 1936, the Communist International formally presented its three-stage plan for achieving world government—Stage 1: socialize the economies of all nations, particularly the Western "capitalistic democracies" (most particularly, the United States); Stage 2: bring about federal unions of various groupings of these socialized nations; Stage 3: amalgamate all of the federal unions into one world-wide union of socialist states. The following passage is from the official program of the 1936 Communist International:

"... dictatorship can be established only by a victory of socialism in different countries or groups of countries, after which the proletariat republics would unite on federal lines with those already in existence, and this system of federal unions would expand ... at length forming the World Union of Socialist Soviet Republics."

In 1939 (three years after this communist program was outlined) Clarence K. Streit (a Rhodes scholar who was foreign correspondent for The New York Times, covering League of Nations activities from 1929-1939) wrote Union Now, a book advocating a gradual approach through regional unions to final world union—an approach identical with that of the communists, except that Streit did not say his scheme was intended to achieve world dictatorship, and did not characterize the end result of his scheme as a "World Union of Socialist Soviet Republics."

$$* \quad * \quad * \quad * \quad *$$

In 1940, Clarence K. Streit (together with Percival F. Brundage, later a Director of the Budget for Eisenhower; and Melvin Ryder, publisher of the Army Times) formed Federal Union, Inc., to work for the goals outlined in Streit's book, Union Now, published the year before.

In 1941, Streit published another book: Union Now With Britain. He claims that the union he advocated would be a step toward "formation of free world government." But the arguments of his book make it very clear that in joining a union with other nations, the United States would not bring to the union old American constitutional concepts of free-enterprise and individual freedom under limited government, but would rather amalgamate with the socialistic-communistic systems that exist in the other nations which became members of the union.

The following passages are from page 192 of Streit's Union Now With Britain:

128

"Democrats cannot . . . quarrel with Soviet Russia or any other nation because of its economic collectivism, for democracy itself introduced the idea of collective machinery into politics. It is a profound mistake to identify democracy and Union necessarily or entirely with either capitalist or socialist society, with either the method of individual or collective enterprise. There is room for both of these methods in democracy . . .

"Democracy not only allows mankind to choose freely between capitalism and collectivism, but it includes marxist governments, parties and press . . ."

When the year 1941 ended, America was in World War II; and all American advocates of world-peace-through-world-law-and-world-government jubilantly struck while the iron was hot—using the hysteria and confusion of the early days of our involvement in the great catastrophe as a means of pushing us into one or another of the schemes for union with other nations.

Clarence Streit states it this way, in his most recent book (Freedom's Frontier Atlantic Union Now, 1961):

"Japan Pearl Harbored us into the war we had sought to avoid by disunion . . . Now, we Americans had the white heat of war to help leaders form the nuclear Atlantic Union."

* * * * *

On January 5, 1942 (when we had been at war less than a month), Clarence Streit's Federal Union, Inc., bought advertising space in major newspapers for a petition urging Congress to adopt a joint resolution favoring immediate union of the United States with several specified foreign nations. Such people as Harold L. Ickes (Roosevelt cabinet officer), Owen J. Roberts (Supreme Court Justice), and John Foster Dulles (later

129

Eisenhower's Secretary of State) signed this newspaper ad petitioning Congress to drag America into world government. In fact, these notables (especially John Foster Dulles) had actually written the Joint Resolution which Federal Union wanted Congress to adopt.

The world government resolution (urged upon Congress in January, 1942) provided among other things that in the federal union of nations to be formed, the "union" government would have the right: (1) to impose a common citizenship; (2) to tax citizens directly; (3) to make and enforce all laws; (4) to coin and borrow money; (5) to have a monopoly on all armed forces; and (6) to admit new members.

The following is from a Federal Union, Inc., ad published in The Washington Evening Star, January 5, 1942, urging upon the people and Congress of America an immediate plunge into world government:

"... Resolved:

"That the President of the United States submit to Congress a program for forming a powerful union of free peoples to win the war, the peace, the future;

"That this program unite our people, on the broad lines of our Constitution, with the people of Canada, the United Kingdom, Eire, Australia, New Zealand, and the Union of South Africa, together with such other free peoples, both in the Old World and the New as may be found ready and able to unite on this federal basis ...

"We gain from the fact that all the Soviet republics are already united in one government, as are also all the Chinese-speaking people, once so divided. Surely, we and they must agree that union now of the democracies wherever possible is equally to the general advantage ...

"Let us begin now a world United States ...

"The surest way to shorten and to win this war is also the surest way to guarantee to ourselves, and our friends and foes, that this war will end in a union of the free. The surest way to do all this is for us to start that union now."

* * * * *

World Fellowship, Inc., was also busy putting pressure on Congress in January, 1942. World Fellowship, Inc., is one of the oldest world government organizations. It was founded in 1918 as the "League of Neighbors."

In 1924, the League of Neighbors united with the Union of East and West (which had been founded in India). In 1933, this combined organization reorganized and changed its name to World Fellowship of Faiths. In late 1941, it changed its name again and incorporated–and has operated since that time as World Fellowship, Inc.

Dr. Willard Uphaus, a notorious communist-fronter, has been Executive Director of World Fellowship, Inc., since February, 1953. Here is a Joint Resolution which World Fellowship, Inc., urged Congress to adopt on or before January 30, 1942–as a birthday present to President Franklin D. Roosevelt.

"Now, therefore, be it

"Resolved by the Senate and House of Representatives of the United States of America, in Congress assembled, That the Congress of the United States of America does hereby solemnly declare that all peoples of the earth should now be united in a commonwealth of nations to be known as the United Nations of the World, and to that end it hereby gives to the President of the United States of America all the needed authority and powers of every kind and description, without limitations of any kind that are necessary in his sole and absolute discretion to set up and create the Federation of the World, a world peace government under the title of the 'United Nations of the World,' including

131

its constitution and personnel and all other matters needed or appertaining thereto to the end that all nations of the world may by voluntary action become a part thereof under the same terms and conditions.

"There is hereby authorised to be appropriated, out of any money in the Treasury not otherwise appropriated, the sum of 100 million dollars or so much thereof as may be necessary, to be expended by the President in his sole and absolute discretion, to effectuate the purposes of this joint resolution, and in addition, the sum of 1 billion dollars for the immediate use of the United Nations of the World under its constitution as set up and created by the President of the United States of America as provided in this joint resolution . . ."

Congress rejected the world-government resolutions urged upon it in 1942 by Federal Union, Inc., and by World Fellowship, Inc.

* * * * *

But the formation of the United Nations in 1945 was a tremendous step in the direction these two organizations were travelling. The "world peace" aspects of the United Nations were emphasized to enlist support of the American public. Few Americans noticed that the UN Charter really creates a worldwide social, cultural, economic, educational, and political alliance—and commits each member nation to a program of total socialism for itself and to the support of total socialism for all other nations.

The United Nations is, to be sure, a weaker alliance than world government advocates want; but the UN was the starting point and framework for world government.

The massive UN propaganda during the first few years after the formation of the UN (1945) was so effective in brainwashing the

American people, that the United World Federalists, beginning with the State Assembly of California, managed to get 27 state legislatures to pass resolutions demanding that Congress call a Constitutional Convention for the purpose of amending our Constitution in order to "expedite and insure" participation of the United States in a world government. When the American people found out what was going on, all of these "resolutions" were repealed–most of them before the end of 1950.

But 1949 was a great year for American world government advocates.

* * * * *

On April 4, 1949, Dean Acheson's "brainchild," the North Atlantic Treaty, was ratified by the United States. President Truman signed the proclamation putting NATO in force on August 24, 1949. Most Americans were happy with this organization. It was supposedly a military alliance to protect the free world against communism. But few Americans bothered to read the brief, 14-article treaty. If they had, Article 2 would have sounded rather strange and out of place in a military alliance. Here is Article 2 of the NATO Treaty:

> "The parties will contribute toward the future development of peaceful and friendly international relations by strengthening their free institutions, by bringing about a better understanding of the principles upon which these institutions are founded, and by promoting conditions of stability and well being. They will seek to eliminate conflict in their international economic policies and will encourage economic collaboration between any or all of them."

Here in this "military" treaty, which re-affirms the participants' "faith in the purposes and principles of the Charter of the United Nations," is the legal basis for a union, an Atlantic Union, a supra-national government, all under the United Nations.

* * * * *

Immediately upon the formation of NATO, Clarence K. Streit created (in 1949) the Atlantic Union Committee, Inc. Strait's old Federal Union was permitted to become virtually defunct (although it technically still exists, as publisher of Streit's books, and so on). Streit got federal tax exemption for the Atlantic Union Committee by writing into its charter a proviso that the organisation would not "attempt to influence legislation by propaganda or otherwise."

Yet, the charter of AUC states its purposes as follows:

"To promote support for congressional action requesting the President of the United States to invite the other democracies which sponsored the North Atlantic Treaty to name delegates, representing their principal political parties, to meet with delegates of the United States in a federal convention to explore how far their peoples, and the peoples of such other democracies as the convention may invite to send delegates, can apply among them, within the framework of the United Nations, the principles of free federal union."

An Atlantic Union Committee Resolution, providing for the calling of an international convention to "explore" steps toward a limited world government, was actually introduced in the Congress in 1949–with the support of a frightful number of "liberals" then in the Congress.

The Resolution did not come to a vote in the 81st Congress (1949-1950). Estes Kefauver (Democrat, Tennessee) gravitated to the leadership in pushing for the Resolution in subsequent Congresses; and he had the support of the top leadership of both parties, Republican and Democrat,

134

north and south–including people like Richard Nixon, William Fulbright, Lister Hill, Hubert Humphrey, Mike Mansfield, Kenneth Keating, Jacob Javits, Christian Herter, and so on.

From 1949 to 1959, the Atlantic Union Resolution was introduced in each Congress–except the one Republican-controlled Congress (83rd–1953).

* * * * *

In 1959, Atlantic Union advocates, having got nowhere in ten years of trying to push their Resolution through Congress, changed tactics. In 1959, Streit's Atlantic Union Committee published a pamphlet entitled, Our One Best Hope–For Us–For The United Nations–For All Mankind, recommending an "action" program to "strengthen the UN." This "action" program asks the U.S. Congress to pass a Resolution calling for an international convention which would accomplish certain "fundamental objectives," to wit:

"That only reasonably experienced democracies be asked to participate; and that the number asked to participate should be small enough to enhance the chance for early agreement, yet large enough to create, if united, a preponderance of power on the side of freedom.

"That the delegates be officially appointed but that they be uninstructed by their governments so that they shall be free to act in accordance with their own individual consciences.

"That, whatever the phraseology, it should not be such as to preclude any proposal which, in the wisdom of the convention, is the most practical step.

"That the findings of the delegates could be only recommendations, later to be accepted or rejected by their legislatures and their fellow citizens."

* * * * *

The NATO Citizens Commission Law of 1960 fully carries out the purposes and intent of the new Atlantic Union strategy fabricated in 1959 to replace the old Resolution which had failed for ten years.

The roll-call vote on this law (published in the February 27, 1961, issue of The Dan Smoot Report) shows what a powerful array of United States Congressmen and Senators are for this step toward world government.

The debates in House and Senate (Senate: Congressional Record, June 15, 1960, pp. 11724 ff; House: Congressional Record, August 24, 1960, pp. 16261 ff) show something even more significant.

While denying that the NATO Citizens Commission Law had any relation to the old Atlantic Union Resolution which Congress had refused for ten years to consider, "liberals" in both Senate and House used language right out of the Atlantic Union Committee pamphlet of 1959 (Our Best Hope . . .) to "prove" that this NATO Citizens Commission proposal was not dangerous: They argued, for example, that Commission members would be free to act in accordance with their own individual consciences; that the meetings of the Commission would be purely exploratory, and that Commission findings would be "only recommendations," not binding on the U.S. government.

Congressional "liberals" supporting the NATO Citizens Commission also tried to establish the respectability of the Commission by arguing that it was merely being created to explore means of implementing Article 2 of the NATO Treaty. Are these "liberal" congressmen and senators so ignorant that they do not know the whole Atlantic Union movement is built under the canopy of "implementing Article 2 of this NATO Treaty?" Or, are they too stupid to understand this? Or, are they so dishonest that they distort the facts, thinking that the public is too confused or ignorant to discover the truth?

Although the liberals in Congress loudly denied that the NATO Citizens Commission Law of 1960 had anything to do with Atlantic

Union, Clarence Streit knew better—or was more honest. As soon as the law was passed, Streit began a hasty revision of his old Union Now. Early in 1961, Harper & Brothers published the revision, under the title Freedom's Frontier Atlantic Union Now.

In this new book, Streit expresses jubilation about the NATO Citizens Commission Law; and, on the second page of the first chapter, he says:

> "One change in the picture, which has seemed too slight or too recent to be noted yet by the general public, seems to me so significant as to give in itself reason enough for new faith in freedom's future, and for this new effort to advance it. On September 7, 1960, President Eisenhower signed an act of Congress authorizing a United States Citizens Commission on NATO to organize and participate in a Convention of Citizens of North Atlantic Democracies with a view to exploring fully and recommending concretely how to unite their peoples better."

The Atlantic Union News (published by the Atlantic Union Committee, Inc.) in the September, 1960, issue presents an exultant article under the headline "AUC Victorious: Resolution Signed by President Becomes Public Law 86-719."

The article says:

> "Members of the Atlantic Union Committee could certainly be forgiven if by now they had decided that the Resolution for an Atlantic Exploratory Convention would never pass both Houses of Congress. However, it has just done so. It was signed into law by the President September 7, 1960. The incredible size of this victory is hard, even for us in Washington, to comprehend . . ."

Who actually runs Clarence Streit's Atlantic Union Committee which finally succeeded in ordering the Congress and the President of the

United States to take this sinister step toward world government? The Council on Foreign Relations! The three top officials of the Atlantic Union Committee are members of the CFR: Elmo Roper, President; William L. Clayton, Vice President; and Lithgow Osborne, Secretary.

As of December, 1960, there were 871 members of the Atlantic Union Committee. Of these, 107 were also members of the Council on Foreign Relations. The December, 1960, membership list of the AUC is in Appendix II of this volume. Each Council on Foreign Relations member is designated on that list with CFR in parentheses after his name.

* * * * *

The NATO Citizens Commission Law of 1960 provided that the Speaker of the House and the Vice President should select 20 persons to serve on the Commission. In March, 1961, Sam Rayburn and Lyndon Johnson appointed the following persons as members of the Commission:

Donald G. Agger; Will L. Clayton; Charles William Engelhard, Jr.; George J. Feldman; Morris Forgash; Christian A. Herter; Dr. Francis S. Hutchins; Eric Johnston; William F. Knowland; Hugh Moore; Ralph D. Pittman, Ben Regan; David Rockefeller; Elmo B. Roper (Jr.); Mrs. Edith S. Sampson; Adolph W. Schmidt; Oliver C. Schroeder; Burr S. Swezey, Sr.; Alex Warden; and Douglas Wynn.

Of the 20 members of the NATO Citizens Commission, 7 are members of the Council on Foreign Relations: Clayton, Herter, Johnston, Moore, Rockefeller, Roper, Schmidt. Roper is President and Clayton is Vice President of the Atlantic Union Committee. The others are generally second-level affiliates of the CFR.

* * * * *

The United World Federalists does not have as much power and influence as Clarence Streit's Atlantic Union, but is clearly the second most influential organization working for world government.

The specific objective of the United World Federalists is rapid transformation (through expansion of the jurisdiction of the World Court, establishment of an international "police force," and so on) of the United Nations into an all-powerful world government.

The aim of the UWF organization, as expressed in its own literature (the most revealing piece of which is a pamphlet called Beliefs, Purposes and Policies) is:

"To create a world federal government with authority to enact, interpret, and enforce world law adequate to maintain peace."

The world federal government would be,

"based upon the following principles and include the following powers . . .

"Membership open to all nations without the right of secession . . . World law should be enforceable directly upon individuals . . . The world government should have direct taxing power independent of national taxation."

The UWF scheme provides for a world police force and the prohibition of "possession by any nation of armaments and forces beyond an approved level required for internal policing."

The UWF proposes to work toward its world government scheme,

"By making use of the amendment process of the United Nations to transform it into such a world federal government;

"By participating in world constituent assemblies, whether of private individuals, parliamentary or other groups seeking to produce draft constitutions for consideration and possible adoption by the United Nations or by national governments . . ."

Norman Cousins and James P. Warburg (both prominent Council on Foreign Relations members) formed the United World Federalists in February, 1947, at Ashville, North Carolina, by amalgamating three small organizations (World Federalists, Student Federalists, and Americans United For World Government).

Cousins is still honorary president of UWF. Walter Reuther (a "second-level" affiliate of the CFR), Cousins, and Warburg actually run the UWF at the top. Other Council on Foreign Relations members who are officials in the UWF include Harry A. Bullis, Arthur H. Bunker, Cass Canfield, Mark F. Ethridge, Douglas Fairbanks, Jr., Harold K. Guinzburg, Isador Lubin, Cord Meyer, Jr., Lewis Mumford, Harry Scherman, Raymond Gram Swing, Paul C. Smith, Walter Wanger, James D. Zellerbach.

* * * * *

The Institute for International Order, 11 West 42nd Street, New York 36, New York, is another organization working for world government. It was founded on November 17, 1948, at Washington, D.C., as the Association for Education in World Government. On May 17, 1952, it changed its name to Institute for International Government. On May 7, 1954, it changed names again, to the present Institute for International Order.

The purpose of this organization has remained constant, through all the name changing, since it was originally founded in 1948: to strengthen the United Nations into a genuine world government. And it is a part of the interlocking apparatus which constitutes our invisible government.

The Institute for International Order gets 75% of its income from foundations which members of the Council on Foreign Relations control; and the following CFR members are officers of the Institute: Earl D.

Osborn (President), Henry B. Cabot (Vice President), Edward W. Barrett, Paul G. Hoffman, and Irving Salomon.

In 1948, the State Department created the U.S. Committee for the UN (mentioned in Chapter VIII, in connection with the Advertising Council) as a semi-official organization to propagandize for the UN in the United States, with emphasis on promoting "UN Day" each year.

The Council on Foreign Relations dominates the U.S. Committee for the UN. Such persons as Stanley C. Allyn, Ralph Bunche, Gardner Cowles, H. J. Heinz, II, Eric Johnston, Milton Katz, Stanley Marcus, Hugh Moore, John Nason, Earl D. Osborn, Jack I. Straus, and Walter Wheeler, Jr.–all Council on Foreign Relations members–are members of the U.S. Committee for the United Nations.

Walter Wheeler, Jr., (last name in the list above) is President of Pitney-Bowes, maker of postage meter machines. In 1961, Mr. Wheeler tried to stop all Pitney-Bowes customers from using, on their meter machines, the American patriotic slogan, "This is a republic, not a democracy: let's keep it that way." Mr. Wheeler said this slogan was controversial. But Mr. Wheeler supported a campaign to get the slogan of international socialism, UN We Believe, used on Pitney-Bowes postage meter machines–probably the most controversial slogan ever to appear in American advertising, as we shall see presently.

The American Association for the United Nations–AAUN–is another tax-exempt, "semi-private" organization set up (not directly by the CFR, but by the State Department which the Council runs) as a propaganda agency for the UN. It serves as an outlet for UN pamphlets and, with chapters in most key cities throughout the United States, as an organizer of meetings, lecture-series, and other programs which propagandize about the ineffable goodness and greatness of the United Nations as the maker and keeper of world peace.

The Council on Foreign Relations dominates the AAUN. Some of the leading CFR members who run the AAUN are: Ralph J. Bunche, Cass Canfield, Benjamin V. Cohen, John Cowles, Clark M. Eichelberger,

Ernest A. Gross, Paul G. Hoffman, Palmer Hoyt, Herbert Lehman, Oscar de Lima, Irving Salomon, James T. Shotwell, Sumner Welles, Quincy Wright.

* * * * *

In 1958, the United States Committee for the UN created an Industry Participation Division for the specific purpose of getting the UN emblem and UN We Believe slogan displayed on the commercial vehicles, stationery, business forms, office buildings, flag poles, and advertising layouts of American business firms. The first major firm to plunge conspicuously into this pro-UN propaganda drive was United Air Lines.

W. A. Patterson, President of United, is an official of the Committee For Economic Development, a major Council on Foreign Relations propaganda affiliate, and has served on the Business-Education Committee of the CED. Mr. Patterson had the UN We Believe emblem painted in a conspicuous place on every plane in the United Air Lines fleet. There was a massive protest from Americans who know that the UN is part of the great scheme to destroy America as a free and independent republic. Mr. Patterson had the UN emblems removed from his planes.

* * * * *

In 1961, the American Association for the United Nations and the U. S. Committee for the UN (both enjoying federal tax exemption, as "educational" in the "public interest") created another tax-exempt organization to plaster the UN emblem all over the American landscape.

The new organization is called UN We Believe. Here is an article from the May-June, 1961, issue of Weldwood News, a house organ of United States Plywood Corporation (New York 36, New York):

"A. W. (Al) Teichmeier, USP director of merchandising, is the Company's closest physical link to the United Nations–he's President of UN We Believe.

"UN We Believe, under joint auspices of the American Association for the UN and the U. S. Committee for the UN, is a non-profit, year-round program geared to convince industry, organizations and individuals how important public support can mean in preserving world peace.

"USP uses the seal... (UN emblem and UN We Believe slogan) on its postage meters for all New York mailings. Among some other active companies in the program are CIT, General Telephone, Texaco, American Sugar Refining, P. Lorillard Co., and KLM Dutch Airlines."

Plywood companies (small ones, producing hardwood plywood, if not big ones like USP) have been grievously hurt by the trade and foreign-aid policies which the UN, international-socialist crowd is responsible for.

Lenin is said to have remarked that when it comes time for communists to hang all capitalists, the capitalists will bid against each other for contracts to sell the rope.

The article from Weldwood News, quoted above, was quoted in the July 17, 1961, issue of The Dan Smoot Report. The companies mentioned received some mail, criticizing them for supporting UN We Believe. The Texaco Company denied that it had ever been active in UN We Believe and said that the editor of Weldwood News had apologized for the error in publishing the reference to Texaco and had expressed regret for "the embarrassment caused" Texaco.

While denying support for UN We Believe, however, Mr. Augustus C. Long, Chairman of the Board of Texaco (and a member of the Business Advisory Council) gave unqualified endorsement of the Council on Foreign Relations. In a letter dated August 17, 1961, Mr. Long said:

143

"The Council on Foreign Relations is one of the most effective organizations in this country devoted to spreading information on international problems. The officers and directors of the Council are men of reputation and stature. We believe that the Council through its study groups makes an outstanding contribution to public information concerning foreign policy issues."

CHAPTER 8.

FOREIGN AID

One day in the spring of 1961, a New York lawyer received a long distance telephone call. Concerning this call, the New York Times reported:

> "'This is President Kennedy,' the telephone voice said.
>
> "'The hell you say,' retorted the lawyer. 'I guess that makes me the Prime Minister of England, but what can I do for you?'
>
> "'Nobody's pulling your leg,' the telephone voice said. 'This is President Kennedy all right. I want to talk to you about coming down here to Washington to help me with this long-term foreign aid legislation.'"

One week later, the New York lawyer took an apartment in Washington and, as a member of President Kennedy's "Task Force" on foreign aid, started writing the Foreign Assistance Act of 1961. The lawyer is Theodore Tannenwald, Jr., a member of the Council on Foreign Relations, who wrote many of the foreign aid bills which President Harry Truman presented to Congress and who, during the first Eisenhower term, was assistant director of the Mutual Security Program.

After Mr. Tannenwald and his task force had finished writing the 1961 foreign aid bill, President Kennedy appointed Tannenwald coordinator in charge of "presenting" the bill to committees of the House and Senate.

Three cabinet officers and the Chairman of the Joint Chiefs of Staff took their orders from Mr. Tannenwald, who was, according to the New York Times, "the Administration's composer, orchestrator and conductor of the most important legislative symphony of the Congressional session." With admiration, the Times said:

"Mr. Tannenwald has been a kind of special White House ambassador to Capitol Hill. While the legislative committees struggled with the controversial proposal to by-pass the appropriating process and give the President authority to borrow $8,800,000,000 (8 billion, 800 million) for development lending in the next five years, he was the man in the ante-room empowered to answer questions in the name of the President."

* * * * *

In July, 1961, President Kennedy completed Mr. Tannenwald's foreign aid "orchestra." On July 10, in ceremonies at the White House, the President formally announced creation of the newest foreign-aid propaganda organization, the Citizens Committee for International Development, with Warren Lee Pierson as chairman. Here is the membership of the Citizens Committee for International Development:

Eugenie Anderson (member of the Atlantic Union Committee); William Benton (Chairman of the Board of Encyclopaedia Britannica; member of the Atlantic Union Committee); Everett N. Case (President of Colgate University); O. Roy Chalk (President of the District of Columbia Transit Company); Malcolm S. Forbes (Editor and Publisher of Forbes Magazine); Eleanor Clark French; Albert M. Greenfield (Honorary Chairman of the Board of Bankers Security Corporation, Philadelphia); General Alfred M. Gruenther (President of the American National Red Cross;

member of the Atlantic Union Committee); Murray D. Lincoln (Chairman of Nationwide Insurance Company); Sol M. Linowitz (Chairman of Zerox Corporation); George Meany (President of AFL-CIO); William S. Paley (Chairman of the Board, Columbia Broadcasting System); Warren Lee Pierson (Chairman of the Board, Trans-World Airways); Ross Pritchard (Professor of Political Science, Southwestern University, Memphis); Thomas S. Nichols (Chairman of the Board of Olin Mathieson Chemical Corporation; member of the Atlantic Union Committee); Mrs. Mary G. Roebling (President Of Trenton Trust Company); David Sarnoff (Chairman of Radio Corporation of America); Walter Sterling Surrey (legal consultant, Economic Cooperation Administration); Thomas J. Watson, Jr., (President of International Business Machines Corporation); Walter H. Wheeler, Jr., (President of Pitney-Bowes); James D. Zellerbach (President and Director of Crown-Zellerbach Corporation; Chairman of Fibreboard Products, Inc.; member of the Atlantic Union Committee and United World Federalists); Ezra Zilkha (head of Zilkha & Sons).

Of these 22 people, 12 (including the Chairman) are members of the Council on Foreign Relations: Benton, Case, Gruenther, Paley, Pierson, Pritchard, Nichols, Sarnoff, Surrey, Watson, Wheeler, and Zellerbach.

* * * * *

Heads of the Ford and Rockefeller Foundations attended the White House luncheon when the Committee was formed. Vice President Johnson, Secretary of State Dean Rusk, and Attorney General Robert Kennedy were also present. The President urged each and all to get foundations, business firms, civic organizations, and the people generally, to put pressure on Congress in support of the 1961 foreign aid bill.

147

Within a week after the July 10, White House luncheon meeting (which launched the CFR's foreign aid committee), the President and his high-level aides were talking about a grave crisis in Berlin and about foreign aid as the essential means of "meeting" that crisis.

On July 25, when congressional debates over the foreign aid bill were in a critical stage, President Kennedy spoke to the nation on radio and television, solemnly warning the people that the Berlin situation was dangerous.

Immediate, additional support for the foreign aid bill came from the country's liberal and leftwing forces, who united in a passionate plea—urging the American people to support the President "in this grave hour."

* * * * *

On August 27, an Associated Press release announced that House Leader John W. McCormack (Democrat, Massachusetts), was attempting to enlist the cooperation of 2,400 city mayors in support of a long-range foreign aid bill to meet the President's demands.

McCormack sent the city officials a statement of his views with a cover letter suggesting that the matter be brought to "the attention of citizens of your community through publication in your local newspaper," and, further, urging their "personal endorsement of this bipartisan program through the medium of your local press . . ."

State Department officials scheduled speaking tours throughout the land, and CFR affiliated organizations (like the Councils on World Affairs) started the build-up to provide audiences—all in the interest of "briefing" the American people on the necessity and beauties of foreign aid.

Anyone with sense had to wonder how the giving of American tax money to communist governments in Europe and to socialist governments all over the earth could help us resist communism in Berlin. But with the top leaders in our society (from the President downward to

148

officials in the National Council of Churches) telling us that the survival of our nation depended on the President's getting all the foreign aid "authorization" he wanted—most Americans remained silent, feeling that such consequential and complicated matters should be left in the hands of our chosen leaders.

By the end of August, the Foreign Assistance Act of 1961 had been passed by both houses of Congress; and the Berlin crisis moved from front page lead articles in the nation's newspapers to less important columns.

Thus, in 1961, as always, the foreign aid bill was a special project of our invisible government, the Council on Foreign Relations. And, in 1961, as always, the great, tax-supported propaganda machine used a fear psychology to bludgeon the people into silence and the Congress into obedience.

President Kennedy signed the Act as Public Law 87-195 on September 4, 1961.

* * * * *

Public Law 87-195 authorized $10,253,500,000 (10 billion, 253 million, 500 thousand) in foreign aid: $3,066,500,000 appropriated for the 1962 fiscal year, and $7,187,000,000 Treasury borrowing authorized for the next five years. The law does require the President to obtain annual appropriations for the Treasury borrowing, but permits him to make commitments to lend the money to foreign countries, before he obtains appropriations from Congress.

It was widely reported in the press that Congress had denied the President the long-term borrowing authority he had requested; but the President himself was satisfied. He knew that by promising loans to foreign governments (that is, "committing" the funds in advance of congressional appropriation) he would thus force Congress (in the interest of showing "national unity" and of not "repudiating" our President) to appropriate whatever he promised.

On August 29, the President said:

> "The compromise . . . is wholly satisfactory. It gives the United States Government authority to make commitments for long-term development programs with reasonable assurance that these commitments will be met."

* * * * *

Former Vice President Richard M. Nixon (a member of the CFR) was happy about the 1961 foreign aid bill. On August 29, Nixon, on the ABC radio network, said that he favored such "long-range foreign aid planning, financed through multi-year authorizations and annual appropriations."

Nelson A. Rockefeller, Republican Governor of New York, announced that he too favored "long-range foreign aid planning, financed through multi-year authorizations and annual appropriations"—exactly like Nixon.

Former President Eisenhower was also happy. He, too, said he favored this sort of thing.

Senator J. William Fulbright (Democrat, Arkansas) was almost jubilant: he said Congress for the next five years would be under "strong obligation" to put up the money for whatever the President promises to foreign governments.

All in all, it is improbable that Congress ever passed another bill more destructive of American constitutional principles; more harmful to our nation politically, economically, morally, and militarily; and more helpful to communism-socialism all over the earth—than the Foreign Assistance Act of 1961, which was, from beginning to end, a product of the Council on Foreign Relations.

150

* * * * *

Our foreign aid does grievous harm to the American people by burdening them with excessive taxation, thus making it difficult for them to expand their own economy. This gives government pretext for intervening with more taxation and controls for domestic subsidies.

Furthermore, the money that government takes away from us for foreign aid is used to subsidize our political enemies and economic competitors abroad. Note, for example, the large quantities of agricultural goods which we give every year to communist satellite nations, thus enabling communist governments to control the hungry people of those nations. Note that while we are giving away our agricultural surpluses to communist and socialist nations, we, under the 1961 foreign aid bill (as under previous ones), are subsidizing agricultural production in the underdeveloped countries.

The 1961 foreign aid bill prohibited direct aid to Cuba, but authorized contributions to United Nations agencies, which were giving aid to Cuba.

At a time when the American economy was suffering from the flight of American industry to foreign lands, the 1961 foreign aid bill offered subsidies and investment guarantees to American firms moving abroad.

Our foreign aid enriches and strengthens political leaders and ruling oligarchies (which are often corrupt) in underdeveloped lands; and it does infinite harm to the people of those lands, when it inflates their economy and foists upon them an artificially-produced industrialism which they are not prepared to sustain or even understand.

* * * * *

The basic argument for foreign aid is that by helping the underdeveloped nations develop, we will keep them from falling under the dictatorship of communism. The argument is false and unsound, historically, politically, economically, and morally.

The communists have never subjugated a nation by winning the loyalties of the oppressed and downtrodden. The communists first win the support of liberal-intellectuals, and then use them to subvert and pervert all established mores and ideals and social and political arrangements.

Our foreign aid does not finance freedom in foreign lands; it finances socialism; and a world socialist system is what communists are trying to establish. As early as 1921, Joseph Stalin said that the advanced western nations must give economic aid to other nations in order to socialize their economies and prepare them for integration in the communist's world socialist system.

Socializing the economies of all nations so that all can be merged into a one-world system was the objective of Colonel Edward M. House, who founded the Council on Foreign Relations, and has been the objective of the Council, and of all its associated organizations, from the beginning.

CHAPTER 9.

MORE OF THE INTERLOCK

It is impossible in this volume to discuss all organizations interlocked with the Council on Foreign Relations. In previous chapters, I have discussed some of the most powerful agencies in the interlock. In this chapter, I present brief discussions of a few organizations which make significant contributions to the over-all program of the Council.

INSTITUTE FOR AMERICAN STRATEGY

There are some men in the Council on Foreign Relations who condemn the consequences of the CFR's policies–but who never mention the CFR as responsible for those policies, and who never really suggest any change in the policies.

Frank R. Barnett is such a man. Mr. Barnett, a member of the Council on Foreign Relations, is research director for the Richardson Foundation and also program director for the Institute for American Strategy, which is largely financed by the Richardson Foundation. The Institute for American Strategy holds two-day regional "Strategy Seminars" in cities throughout the United States. Participants in the seminars are carefully selected civic and community leaders. The announced official purpose of the seminars is:

". . . to inform influential private American citizens of the danger which confronts the United States in the realm of world politics. They have been conceived as a means for arousing an informed and articulate patriotism which can provide the basis for the sustained and intensive effort which alone can counter the skillful propaganda and ruthless conquest so successfully practiced by the Soviet Union and her allies and satellites."

Mr. Barnett is generally one of the featured speakers at these seminars. He speaks effectively, arousing his audience to an awareness of the Soviets as an ugly menace to freedom and decency in the world. He makes his audience squirm with anxiety about how America is losing the cold war on all fronts, and makes them burn with desire to reverse this trend. But when it comes to suggesting what can be done about the terrible situation, Mr. Barnett seems only to recommend that more and more people listen to more and more speakers like him in order to become angrier at the Soviets and more disturbed about American losses—so that we can continue the same policies we have, but do a better job with them.

Mr. Barnett never criticizes the basic internationalist policy of entwining the affairs of America with those of other nations, because Mr. Barnett, like all other internationalists, takes it for granted that America can no longer defend herself, without "allies," whom we must buy with foreign aid. He does imply that our present network of permanent, entangling alliances is not working well; but he never hints that we should abandon this disastrous policy and return to the traditional American policy of benign neutrality and no-permanent-involvement, which offers the only possible hope for our peace and security. Rather, Mr. Barnett would just like us to conduct our internationalist policy in such a way as to avoid the disaster which our internationalist policy is building for us.

* * * * *

Mr. Barnett's recommendations on how to fight communism on the domestic front also trail off, generally, into contradictions and confusion. For example, in his speech to the "Strategy Seminar" arranged by the Institute for American Strategy and sponsored by the Fulton County Medical Society in Atlanta, Georgia, June, 1961, Mr. Barnett urged all citizens to inform themselves about the communist threat and become educated on its aims so that they will be capable of combatting communist propaganda. But, Mr. Barnett said, citizens are "silly" who concern themselves with trying to find communists and fellow-travelers in the PTA!

In a speech to reserve officers at the War College in July, 1961, Mr. Barnett denounced "crackpots" who hunt "pinkos" in local colleges. He said the theory that internal subversion is the chief danger to the United States is fallacious—and is harmful, because it has great popular appeal. Belief in this theory, Mr. Barnett said, makes people mistakenly feel that they "don't have to think about . . . strengthening NATO, or improving foreign aid management, or volunteering for the Peace Corps, or anything else that might require sacrifice."

Mr. Barnett, who speaks persuasively as an expert on fighting communism, apparently does not know that the real work of the communist conspiracy is not performed by the shabby people who staff the official apparatus of the communist party, but is done by well-intentioned people (in the PTA and similar organizations) who have been brainwashed with communist ideas. Communists (whom Mr. Barnett hates and fears) did not do the tremendous job of causing the United States to abandon her traditional policies of freedom and independence for the internationalist policies which are dragging us into one-world socialism. The most distinguished and respected Americans of our time, in the Council on Foreign Relations (of which Mr. Barnett is a member) did this job.

It is interesting to note that the principal book offered for sale and recommended for reading at Mr. Barnett's, "Strategy Seminars" is

American Strategy For The Nuclear Age. The first chapter in the book, entitled "Basic Aims of United States Foreign Policy," is a reprint of a Council on Foreign Relations report, compiled by a CFR meeting in 1959, attended by such well-known internationalist "liberals" as Frank Altschul, Hamilton Fish Armstrong, Adolf A. Berle, Jr., Robert Blum, Robert R. Bowie, John Cowles, Arthur H. Dean, Thomas K. Finletter, William C. Foster, W. Averell Harriman, Philip C. Jessup, Joseph E. Johnson, Henry R. Luce, I. I. Rabi, Herman B. Wells, Henry M. Wriston.

COMMISSION ON NATIONAL GOALS

On December 6, 1960, President Eisenhower presented, to President-elect Kennedy, a report by the President's Commission on National Goals, a group of "distinguished" Americans whom President Eisenhower had appointed 11 months before to find out what America's national purpose should be.

The national purpose of this nation should be exactly what it was during the first 125 years of our national life: to stand as proof that free men can govern themselves; to blaze a trail toward freedom, a trail which all people, if they wish, can follow or guide themselves by, without any meddling from us.

Hydrogen bombs and airplanes and intercontinental ballistic missiles do not change basic principles. The principles on which our nation was founded are eternal, as valid now as in the 18th century.

Indeed, modern developments in science should make us cling to those principles. If foreign enemies can now destroy our nation by pressing a button, it seems obvious that our total defense effort should be devoted to protecting our nation against such an attack: it is suicidal for us to waste any of our defense effort on "economic improvement" and military assistance for other nations.

All of this being obvious, it is also obvious that the President's Commission on National Goals was not really trying to discover our "national purpose." "National Purpose" was the label for a propaganda effort intended to help perpetuate governmental policies, which are dragging America into international socialism, regardless of who succeeded Eisenhower as President.

The Report is actually a rehash of major provisions in the 1960 Democrat and Republican party platforms. More than that, it is, in several fundamental and specific ways, identical with the 1960 published program of the communist party. (For a full discussion of the President's Commission on National Goals, see The Dan Smoot Report, "Our National Purpose," December 12, 1960.)

Who were the "distinguished" Americans whom Eisenhower appointed to draw this blueprint of America's National Purpose? They were:

Erwin D. Canham, Editor-in-Chief of the Christian Science Monitor; James B. Conant, former President of Harvard; Colgate W. Darden, Jr., former President of the University of Virginia and former Governor of Virginia; Crawford H. Greenewalt, President of E. I. du Pont de Nemours & Co., Inc.; General Alfred M. Gruenther, President of the American Red Cross; Learned Hand, retired judge of the U.S. Court of Appeals; Clark Kerr, President of the University of California; James R. Killian, Jr., Chairman of the Massachusetts Institute of Technology; George Meany, President of the AFL-CIO; Frank Pace, Jr., former member of Truman's cabinet; Henry M. Wriston, President of American Assembly and President Emeritus of Brown University.

Of the 11, 7 are members of the Council on Foreign Relations—Canham, Conant, Gruenther, Hand, Killian, Pace, Wriston. All of the others are lower-level affiliates of the CFR.

NATIONAL PLANNING ASSOCIATION

The National Planning Association was established in 1934 "to bring together leaders from agriculture, business, labor, and the professions to pool their experience and foresight in developing workable plans for the nation's future . . ."

The quotation is from an NPA booklet, which also says:

"Every year since the NPA was organized in 1934, its reports have strongly influenced our national economy, U.S. economic policy, and business decisions."

Here are members of the Council on Foreign Relations listed as officials of the National Planning Association: Frank Altschul, Laird Bell, Courtney C. Brown, Eric Johnston, Donald R. Murphy, Elmo Roper, Beardsley Ruml, Hans Christian Sonne, Lauren Soth, Wayne Chatfield Taylor, John Hay Whitney.

The following officials of National Planning Association are generally second-level affiliates of the CFR–or are, at any rate, worth noting: Arnold Zander, International President of American Federation of State, County and Municipal Employees; Solomon Barkin, Director of Research for the Textile Workers Union of America; L. S. Buckmaster, General President, United Rubber, Cork, Linoleum & Plastic Workers of America; James B. Carey, Secretary-Treasurer of CIO; Albert J. Hayes, International President of International Association of Machinists; and Walter P. Reuther.

AMERICAN CIVIL LIBERTIES UNION

In 1920, the American Civil Liberties Union was founded by Felix Frankfurter, a member of the Council on Foreign Relations, William Z. Foster, then head of the U.S. Communist Party; Elizabeth Gurley Flynn, a top communist party official; Dr. Harry F. Ward, of Union Theological Seminary, a notorious communist-fronter; and Roger Baldwin.

Patrick M. Malin, a member of the CFR, has been director of the American Civil Liberties Union since 1952. Other CFR members who are known to be officials in the American Civil Liberties Union are: William Butler, Richard S. Childs, Norman Cousins, Palmer Hoyt, Jr., J. Robert Oppenheimer, Elmo Roper, Arthur M. Schlesinger, Jr.

NATIONAL CONFERENCE OF CHRISTIANS AND JEWS

The late Charles Evans Hughes (a member of the CFR) and the late S. Parkes Cadman (former President of the Federal–now National–Council of Churches) founded the National Conference of Christians and Jews in 1928.

In June, 1950 (at the suggestion of Paul Hoffman) the National Conference of Christians and Jews founded World Brotherhood at UNESCO House in Paris, France. The officers of World Brotherhood were: Konrad Adenauer, William Benton, Arthur H. Compton, Paul Henri-Spaak, Paul G. Hoffman, Herbert H. Lehman, John J. McCloy, George Meany, Madame Pandit, Paul Reynaud, Eleanor Roosevelt, Adlai Stevenson.

* * * * *

In August, 1958, World Brotherhood held a seminar in Bern, Switzerland. All of the officers listed above attended and prepared "working papers." Here is a summary of conclusions reached at this World Brotherhood meeting, as condensed from an article by Arthur Krock, in The New York Times, November 21, 1958:

> We must recognize that the communist countries are here to stay and cannot be wished away by propaganda. All is not bad in communist countries. Western nations could learn from communist experiments. We should study ways to make changes in both systems–communist and western–in order to bring them nearer together. We should try to eliminate the stereo-type attitudes

about, and suspicion of, communism. We must assume that the communist side is not worse than, but merely different from, our side.

In May, 1960, World Brotherhood held a conference on "World Tensions" at Chicago University. Lester B. Pearson (socialist-internationalist from Canada) presided at the conference; and the following members of the Council on Foreign Relations served as officials: William Benton, Ralph Bunche, Marquis Childs, Harlan Cleveland, Norman Cousins, Ernest A. Gross, Paul G. Hoffman, and Adlai Stevenson.

The National Conference of Christians and Jews-World Brotherhood 1960 meeting on "World Tensions," at Chicago University, concluded that the communists are interested in more trade but not interested in political subversion, and recommended:

(1) a three-billion-dollar-a-year increase in U. S. foreign aid to "poor" countries; (2) repeal of the Connally Reservation; (3) closer relations between the U. S. and communist countries.

Adlai Stevenson told the group that Khrushchev is merely a "tough and realistic politician and polemicist," with whom it is possible to "conduct the dialogue of reason."

* * * * *

In 1961, World Brotherhood, Inc., changed its name to Conference On World Tensions.

AMERICAN ASSEMBLY

In 1950, when President of Columbia University, General Dwight D. Eisenhower founded the American Assembly—sometimes calling itself the Arden House Group, taking this name from its headquarters and meeting place. The Assembly holds a series of meetings at Arden

House in New York City about every six months, and other round-table discussions at varying intervals throughout the nation.

The 19th meeting of the Arden House Group, which ended May 7, 1961, was typical of all others, in that it was planned and conducted by members of the Council on Foreign Relations—and concluded with recommendations concerning American policy, which, if followed, would best serve the ends of the Kremlin.

This 1961 Arden House meeting dealt with the problem of disarmament. Henry M. Wriston (President of American Assembly and Director of the Council on Foreign Relations) presided over the three major discussion groups—each group, in turn, was under the chairmanship of a member of the Council: Raymond J. Sontag of the University of California; Milton Katz, Director of International Legal Studies at Harvard; and Dr. Philip E. Mosely, Director of Studies for the Council on Foreign Relations.

John J. McCloy (a member of the CFR) as President Kennedy's Director of Disarmament, sent three subordinates to participate. Two of the three (Edmund A. Gullion, Deputy Director of the Disarmament Administration; and Shepard Stone, a Ford Foundation official) are members of the CFR.

Here are two major recommendations which the May, 1961, American Assembly meeting made:

(1) that the United States avoid weapons and measures which might give "undue provocation" to the Soviets, and which might reduce the likelihood of disarmament agreements;

(2) that the United States strengthen its conventional military forces for participation in "limited wars" but avoid building up an ordnance of nuclear weapons.

We cannot match the communist nations in manpower or "conventional military forces" and should not try. Our only hope is to

161

keep our military manpower in reserve, and uncommitted, in the United States, while building an overwhelming superiority in nuclear weapons. When we "strengthen our conventional forces for participation in limited wars," we are leaving the Soviets with the initiative to say when and where those wars will be fought; and we are committing ourselves to fight with the kind of forces in which the Soviets will inevitably have superiority. More than that, we are consuming so much of our economic resources that we do not have enough left for weaponry of the kind that would defend our homeland.

AMERICANS FOR DEMOCRATIC ACTION

The ADA was founded in April, 1947, at a meeting in the old Willard Hotel, Washington, D. C. Members of the Council on Foreign Relations dominated this meeting–and have dominated the ADA ever since.

Here are members of the Council on Foreign Relations who are, or were, top officials in Americans For Democratic Action: Francis Biddle, Chester Bowles, Marquis Childs, Elmer Davis, William H. Davis, David Dubinsky, Thomas K. Finletter, John Kenneth Galbraith, Palmer Hoyt, Hubert H. Humphrey, Jacob K. Javits, Herbert H. Lehman, Reinhold Niebuhr, Arthur Schlesinger, Jr.

Here are some of the policies which the ADA openly and vigorously advocated in 1961:

Abolition of the House Committee on Un-American Activities
Congressional investigation of the John Birch Society
Total Disarmament under United Nations control
U. S. recognition of red China
Admission of red China to the United Nations, in place of nationalist China
Federal aid to all public schools

162

Drastic overhaul of our immigration laws, to permit a more
  "liberal" admission of immigrants
Urban renewal and planning for all cities

* * * * *

Here is a good, brief characterization of the ADA, from a Los Angeles
Times editorial, September 18, 1961:

"The ADA members . . . are as an organization strikingly
like the British Fabian Socialists . . . The Fabians stood for non-
Marxian evolutionary socialism, to be achieved not by class war
but by ballot . . .

"ADA is not an organization for subversive violence like
Marxist-Lenin communism . . . The socialism they want to bring
about would be quite as total, industrially, as that in Russia, but they
would accomplish it by legislation, not by shooting, and, of course,
by infiltrating the executive branch of the government . . ."

SANE NUCLEAR POLICY, INC.

In 1955, Bertrand Russell (British pro-communist socialist) and the
late Albert Einstein (notorious for the number of communist fronts
he supported) held a meeting in London (attended by communists and
socialists from all over the world). In a fanfare of publicity, Russell and
Einstein demanded international co-operation among atomic scientists.

Taking his inspiration from this meeting, Cyrus Eaton (wealthy
American industrialist, notorious for his consistent pro-communist
sympathies), in 1956, held the first "Pugwash Conference," which was a
gathering of pro-Soviet propagandists, called scientists, from red China,
the Soviet Union, and Western nations.

Another Pugwash Conference was held in 1957; and from these Pugwash Conferences, the idea for a Sane Nuclear Policy, Inc., emerged.

* * * * *

Sane Nuclear Policy, Inc., was founded in November, 1957, with national headquarters in New York City, and with Bertrand Russell of England and Swedish socialist Gunnar Myrdal (among others) as honorary sponsors.

Officers of Sane Nuclear Policy, Inc., are largely second-level affiliates of the Council on Foreign Relations, with a good representation from the CFR itself. Here are past and present officials of SANE, who are also members of the Council on Foreign Relations: Harry A. Bullis, Henry Seidel Canby, Norman Cousins, Clark M. Eichelberger, Lewis Mumford, Earl D. Osborn, Elmo Roper, James T. Shotwell, James P. Warburg.

Other national officials of SANE, who are not members of the CFR, but worthy of note, are: Steve Allen, Harry Belafonte, Walt Kelly, Martin Luther King, Linus Pauling, Norman Thomas, Bruno Walter.

A typical activity of SANE was a public rally at Madison Square Garden in New York City on May 19, 1960, featuring speeches by Eleanor Roosevelt, Walter Reuther, Norman Thomas, Alf Landon, Israel Goldstein, and G. Mennen Williams. All speakers demanded disarmament and strengthening the United Nations until it becomes strong enough to maintain world peace.

Commenting on this SANE rally at Madison Square Garden, Senator James O. Eastland, Chairman of the Senate Internal Security Subcommittee said (in a press release from his office, dated October 12, 1960):

> "The communists publicized the meeting well in advance through their own and sympathetic periodicals . . . The affair, in Madison Square Garden May 19, was sponsored by the Committee for a

Sane Nuclear Policy . . . Chief organizer of the Garden meeting, however, was one Henry H. Abrams of 11 Riverside Drive, New York, New York, who was a veteran member of the communist party . . . It is to the credit of the officers of the organization that, when Abrams' record of communist connections was brought to their attention, Abrams was immediately discharged."

FREE EUROPE COMMITTEE

The Free Europe Committee, Inc., was founded in New York, primarily by Herbert H. Lehman (then United States Senator) in 1949. Its revenue comes from the big foundations (principally, Ford) and from annual fund-raising drives conducted in the name of Crusade for Freedom. The main activity of The Free Europe Committee (apart from the fund raising) is the running of Radio Free Europe and Free Europe Press.

Every year, Crusade for Freedom (with major assistance from Washington officialdom) conducts a vigorous nationwide drive, pleading for "truth dollars" from the American people to finance the activities of Radio Free Europe and Free Europe Press, which are supposed to be fighting communism behind the iron curtain by spreading the truth about communism to people in the captive satellite nations.

It is widely known among well-informed anti-communists, however, that Radio Free Europe actually helps, rather than hurts, the cause of international communism–particularly in the captive nations.

Radio Free Europe broadcasts tell the people behind the iron curtain that communism is bad–as if they did not know this better than the RFE broadcasters do; but the broadcasts consistently support the programs, and present the ideology, of international socialism, always advocating the equivalent of a one-world socialist society as the solution to all problems. This is, of course, the communist solution. And it is also the solution desired by the Council on Foreign Relations.

A bill of particulars which reveals that Radio Free Europe helps rather than hurts communism with its so-called "anti-communist" broadcasts can be found in the Congressional Record for June 20, 1956. An article, beginning on page A4908, was put in the Record by former Congressman Albert H. Bosch, of New York. It was written by George Brada, a Czechoslovakian who fled his homeland after the communists had taken over in 1948. Brada now lives in Western Germany and is active in a number of anti-communist groups in Western Europe.

In reality, the Free Europe Committee and its subsidiary organizations constitute another propaganda front for the Council on Foreign Relations. Here, for example, are the CFR members who are, or have been, top officials of Free Europe Committee, Crusade for Freedom, or Radio Free Europe—or all three: Adolf A. Berle, David K. E. Bruce, General Lucius D. Clay, Will L. Clayton, Allen W. Dulles, Dwight D. Eisenhower, Mark F. Ethridge, Julius Fleischmann, Henry Ford II, Walter S. Gifford, Joseph C. Grew, Palmer Hoyt, C. D. Jackson, Herbert H. Lehman, Henry R. Luce, Edward R. Murrow, Irving S. Olds, Arthur W. Page, David Sarnoff, Whitney H. Shepardson, George N. Shuster, Charles M. Spofford, Harold E. Stassen, H. Gregory Thomas, Walter H. Wheeler, Jr.

NATIONAL ASSOCIATION FOR THE ADVANCEMENT OF COLORED PEOPLE

The Council on Foreign Relations has had a strong (though, probably, not controlling) hand in the NAACP. Felix Frankfurter, CFR member, was an attorney for the NAACP for ten years. Other CFR members who are, or were, officials of the NAACP: Ralph Bunche, Norman Cousins, Lewis S. Gannett, John Hammond, Herbert H. Lehman.

AMERICAN COMMITTEE ON AFRICA

The American Committee on Africa is a propaganda agency which concentrates on condemning the apartheid policies of the government of the Union of South Africa–a nation of white people (practically encircled by millions of black savages), who feel that their racial policies are their only hope of avoiding total submergence and destruction. In addition to disseminating propaganda to create ill-will for South Africa among Americans, the American Committee on Africa gives financial assistance to agitators and revolutionaries in the Union of South Africa.

It has, for example, given financial aid to 156 persons charged with treason under the laws of the Union.

Here are some of the Council on Foreign Relations members who are officials of the American Committee on Africa: Gardner Cowles, Lewis S. Gannett, John Gunther, Senator Hubert H. Humphrey, Dr. Robert L. Johnson, Dr. Reinhold Niebuhr, Arthur M. Schlesinger, Jr. Mrs. Chester Bowles is also an official.

WORLD POPULATION EMERGENCY CAMPAIGN

The World Population Emergency Campaign urges the United States government to use American tax money in an effort to solve the world population problem. It specifically endorses the 1959 Draper Report on foreign aid, which recommended that the United States appropriate money for a United Nations population control project.

Leadership of the World Population Emergency Campaign is dominated by such CFR members as: Will L. Clayton, Lammot DuPont Copeland, Major General William H. Draper, John Nuveen. Most of the members of the "Campaign" also belong to the Atlantic Union Committee, or to some other second-level affiliate of the CFR.

SCHOOL OF INTERNATIONAL SERVICE

The School of International Service at American University in Washington, D. C., initiated a new academic program to train foreign service officers and other officials in newly independent nations, commencing in September, 1961. The foreign diplomats will study courses on land reforms, finance, labor problems, and several courses on Soviet and Chinese communism. The program (under the newly created Center of Diplomacy and Foreign Policy) is directed by former Under Secretary of State Loy W. Henderson, a member of the Council on Foreign Relations.

INSTITUTE OF INTERNATIONAL EDUCATION

In 1919, Elihu Root and Stephen Duggan (both members of the Council on Foreign Relations) founded the Institute of International Education, to develop international understanding and goodwill through exchange of students, teachers, and others in the educational field.

Prior to World War II, the Institute was financed by the Carnegie Corporation. Since the War, the federal government has contributed a little more than one-third of the Institute's annual income of about 1.8 million dollars. Foundations, corporations, individuals, and colleges, contribute the rest.

The Institute is wholly a CFR operation. Its officials are: Stanley C. Allyn, Edward W. Barrett, Chester Bowles, Ralph J. Bunche, William C. Foster, Arthur A. Houghton, Grayson L. Kirk, Edward R. Murrow, George N. Shuster, and James D. Zellerbach—all members of the CFR.

CHAPTER 10.

COMMUNICATIONS MEDIA

In nine chapters of this Volume, I have managed to discuss only a few of the most powerful organizations interlocked with the Council on Foreign Relations, to form an amazing web which is the invisible government of the United States. There are scores of such organizations.

I have managed to name, relatively, only a few of the influential individuals who are members of the Council on Foreign Relations, or of affiliated agencies, and who also occupy key jobs in the executive branch of government, including the Presidency.

I have asserted that the objective of the invisible government is to convert America into a socialist nation and then make it a unit in a one-world socialist system.

The managers of the combine do not admit this, of course. They are "liberals" who say that the old "negative" kind of government we used to have is inadequate for this century. The liberals' "positive" foreign policy is said to be necessary for "world peace" and for meeting "America's responsibility" in the world. Their "positive" domestic policies are said to be necessary for the continued improvement and progress of our "free-enterprise" system.

But the "positive" foreign policy for peace has dragged us into so many international commitments (many of which are in direct conflict with each other: such as, our subsidizing national independence for former colonies of European powers, while we are also subsidizing the European powers trying to keep the colonies) that, if we continue in our present direction, we will inevitably find ourselves in perpetual war for perpetual peace–or we will surrender our freedom and national independence and become an out-voted province in a socialist one-world system.

The liberals' "positive" domestic policies always bring the federal government into the role of subsidizing and controlling the economic activities of the people; and that is the known highway to the total, tyrannical socialist state.

The Council on Foreign Relations is rapidly achieving its purpose. An obvious reason for its success: it is reaching the American public with its clever propaganda.

However much power the CFR combine may have inside the agencies of government; however extensive the reach of its propaganda through organizations designed to "educate" the public to acceptance of CFR ideas–the CFR needs to reach the mass audience of Americans who do not belong to, or attend the meetings of, or read material distributed by, the propaganda organizations. Council on Foreign Relations leaders are aware of this need, and they have met it.

*　*　*　*　*

In the 1957 Annual Report of the Committee for Economic Development (a major propaganda arm of the CFR), Gardner Cowles, then Chairman of CED's Information Committee, did a bit of boasting about how successful CED had been in communicating its ideas to the general public. Mr. Cowles said:

> "The value of CED's research and recommendations is directly related to its ability to communicate them . . . the organization's role as an agency that can influence private and public economic policies and decisions . . . can be effective . . . only to the extent that CED gets its ideas across to thinking people . . .

"During the year [1957], the Information Division [of CED] distributed 42 pamphlets having a total circulation of 545,585; issued 37 press releases and texts of statements; arranged 4 press conferences, 10 radio and television appearances, 12 speeches for Trustees, 3 magazine articles and the publication of 3 books . . . In assessing the year, we are reminded again of the great debt we owe the nation's editors. Their regard for the objectivity and non-partisanship of CED's work is reflected in the exceptional attention they give to what CED has to say. The [CED] statement, 'Toward a Realistic Farm Policy,' for example not only received extended news treatment but was the subject of 362 editorials. The circulation represented in the editorials alone totaled 19,336,299."

Mr. Cowles was modest. He gave only a hint of the total extent to which the mass-communication media have become a controlled propaganda network for the Council on Foreign Relations and its inter-connecting agencies.

I doubt that anyone really knows the full extent. My research reveals a few of the CFR members who have (or have had) controlling, or extremely influential, positions in the publishing and broadcasting industries. My list of CFR members in this field is far from complete; and I have not tried to compile a list of the thousands of people who are not members of the CFR, but who are members of CED, FPA, or of some other CFR affiliate—and who also control important channels of public communications.

Hence, the following list—of Council on Foreign Relations members whom I know to be influential in the communications industries—is intended to be indicative, rather than comprehensive and informative:

Herbert Agar (former Editor, Louisville Courier-Journal)

Hanson W. Baldwin (Military Affairs Editor, New York Times)

Joseph Barnes (Editor-in-Chief, Simon & Schuster, Publishers)

Elliott V. Bell (Chairman of Executive Committee, McGraw-Hill Publishing Co.; Publisher and Editor of Business Week)

John Mason Brown (Editor, Saturday Review of Literature, drama critic, author)

Cass Canfield (Chairman of the Editorial Board of Harper & Brothers, Publishers)

Marquis Childs (author, syndicated columnist)

Norman Cousins (Editor-in-Chief, Saturday Review of Literature)

Gardner Cowles, quoted above from the 1957 CED Annual Report, and John Cowles (They occupy controlling offices in Cowles Magazine Company, which owns such publications as Look, Minneapolis Star and Tribune, and Des Moines Register and Tribune, and which also owns a broadcasting company.)

Mark Ethridge (Publisher, Louisville Courier-Journal, Louisville Times)

George Gallup (public opinion analyst, Gallup Poll; President, National Municipal League)

Philip Graham (Publisher, Washington Post and Times Herald)

Allen Grover (Vice President of Time, Inc.)

Joseph C. Harsch (of The Christian Science Monitor)

August Heckscher (Editor, New York Herald Tribune)

Palmer Hoyt (Publisher, Denver Post)

David Lawrence (President and Editor-in-Chief, U. S. News and World Report)

Hal Lehrman (Editor, New York Post)

Irving Levine (NBC news official and commentator)

172

Walter Lippmann (author, syndicated columnist)

Henry R. Luce (Publisher, Time, Life, Fortune, Sports Illustrated)

Malcolm Muir (Chairman of the Board and Editor-in-Chief, Newsweek)

William S. Paley (Chairman of the Board, Columbia Broadcasting System)

Ogden Reid (former Chairman of the Board, New York Herald Tribune)

Whitelaw Reid (former Editor-in-Chief, New York Herald Tribune)

James B. Reston (Editorial writer, New York Times)

Elmo Roper (public opinion analyst, Roper Poll)

David Sarnoff (Chairman of the Board, Radio Corporation of America–NBC, RCA Victor, etc.)

Harry Scherman (founder and Chairman of the Board, Book-of-the-Month Club)

William L. Shirer (author, news commentator)

Paul C. Smith (President and Editor-in-Chief, Crowell-Collier Publishing Company)

Leland Stone (head of News Reporting for Radio Free Europe, Chicago Daily News foreign correspondent)

Robert Kenneth Straus (former research director for F. D. Roosevelt's Council of Economic Advisers; owner and publisher of the San Fernando, California, Sun; largest stockholder and member of Board of Orange Coast Publishing Company, which publishes the Daily Globe-Herald of Costa Mesa, the Pilot and other small newspapers in California; member of group which owns and publishes American Heritage and Horizon magazines; Treasurer and Director of Industrial Publishing Company of Cleveland, which publishes trade magazines)

Arthur Hayes Sulzberger (Chairman of the Board, New York Times)

C. L. Sulzberger (Editorial writer, New York Times)

I do not mean to imply that all of these people are controlled by the Council on Foreign Relations, or that they uniformly support the total program of international socialism which the Council wants. The Council does not own its members: it merely has varying degrees of influence on each.

For example, former President Herbert Hoover, a member of the Council, has fought eloquently against many basic policies which the Council supports. Spruille Braden is another.

Mr. Braden formerly held several important ambassadorial posts and at one time was Assistant Secretary of State in charge of American Republic Affairs. In recent years, Mr. Braden has given leadership to many patriotic organizations and efforts, such as For America and The John Birch Society; and, in testimony before various committees of Congress, he has given much valuable information about communist influences in the State Department.

Mr. Braden joined the Council on Foreign Relations in the late 1920's or early 30's, when membership in the Council was a fashionable badge of respectability, helpful to the careers of young men in the foreign service, in the same way that membership in expensive country clubs and similar organizations is considered helpful to the careers of young business executives.

Men who know Braden well say that he stayed in the Council after he came to realize its responsibility for the policies of disaster which our nation has followed in the postwar era—hoping to exert some pro-American influence inside the Council.

It apparently was a frustrated hope. There is a story in well-informed New York circles about the last time the Council on Foreign Relations ever called on Spruille Braden to participate in an important activity. Braden

174

was asked to preside over a Council on Foreign Relations meeting when the featured speaker was Herbert Matthews (member of the New York Times editorial board) whose support of communist Castro in Cuba is notorious. It is said that the anti-communist viewpoint which Braden tried to inject into this meeting will rather well guarantee against his ever being asked to officiate at another CFR affair.

Generally, however, the degree of influence which the CFR exerts upon its own members is very high indeed.

* * * * *

Apart from an occasional article or editorial which criticizes some aspect of, or some leader in, the socialist revolution in America; and despite much rhetoric in praise of "free enterprise" and "the American way," such publications as Time, Life, Fortune, New York Times, New York Post, Louisville Courier-Journal, Washington Post and Times Herald, Saturday Review of Literature, the Denver Post, The Christian Science Monitor and Look (I name only those, in the list above, which I, personally, have read a great deal.) have not one time in the past 15 years spoken editorially against any fundamentally important aspect of the over-all governmental policies which are dragging this nation into socialism and world government—at least, not to my knowledge.

On the contrary, these publications heartily support those policies, criticizing them, if at all, only about some detail—or for being too timid, small and slow!

In contrast, David Lawrence, of U. S. News & World Report, publishes fine, objective news-reporting, often featuring articles which factually expose the costly fallacies of governmental policy. This is especially true of U. S. News & World Report in connection with domestic issues. On matters of foreign policy, David Lawrence often goes down the line for the internationalist policy—being convinced (as all internationalists seem to be) that this is the only policy possible for America in the "shrunken world" of the twentieth century.

An intelligent man like David Lawrence–who must see the endless and unbroken chain of disasters which the internationalist foreign policy has brought to America; and who is thoroughly familiar with the proven record of marvelous success which our traditional policy of benign neutrality and no-permanent-involvement enjoyed: how can he still feel that we are nonetheless inescapably bound to follow the policy of disaster? I wish I knew.

CHAPTER 11.

INTERLOCKING UNTOUCHABLES

Members of Congress are not unaware of the far-reaching power of the tax-exempt private organization—the CFR; but the power of the Council is somewhat indicated by the fact that no committee of Congress has yet been powerful enough to investigate it or the foundations with which it has interlocking connections and from which it receives its support.

On August 1, 1951, Congressman E. E. Cox (Democrat, Georgia) introduced a resolution in the House asking for a Committee to conduct a thorough investigation of tax-exempt foundations. Congressman Cox said that some of the great foundations,

"had operated in the field of social reform and international relations (and) many have brought down on themselves harsh and just condemnation."

He named the Rockefeller Foundation,

"whose funds have been used to finance individuals and organizations whose business it has been to get communism into the private and public schools of the country, to talk down America and to play up Russia."

He cited the Guggenheim Foundation, whose money,

"was used to spread radicalism throughout the country to an extent not excelled by any other foundation."

He listed the Carnegie Corporation, The Rosenwald Fund, and other foundations, saying:

"There are disquieting evidences that at least a few of the foundations have permitted themselves to be infiltrated by men and women who are disloyal to our American way of life. They should be investigated and exposed to the pitiless light of publicity, and appropriate legislation should be framed to correct the present situation."

Congressman Cox's resolution, proposing an investigation of foundations, died in Committee.

* * * * *

On March 10, 1952, Cox introduced the same resolution again. Because he had mentioned foundation support for Langston Hughes, a Negro communist, Congressman Cox was accused of racial prejudice. Because he had criticized the Rosenwald Fund for making grants to known communists, he was called anti-semitic. But the Cox resolution was adopted in 1952; and the Cox committee to investigate tax-exempt foundations was set up.

Congressman Cox died before the end of the year; and the final report of his committee (filed January 1, 1953) was a pathetic whitewash of the whole subject.

A Republican-controlled Congress (the 83rd) came into existence in January, 1953.

178

* * * * *

On April 23, 1953, the late Congressman Carroll Reece, (Republican, Tennessee) introduced a resolution proposing a committee to carry on the "unfinished business" of the defunct Cox Committee. The new committee to investigate tax-exempt foundations (popularly known as the Reece Committee) was approved by Congress on July 27, 1953. It went out of existence on January 3, 1955, having proven, mainly, that the mammoth tax-exempt foundations have such power in the White House, in Congress, and in the press that they are quite beyond the reach of a mere committee of the Congress of the United States.

If you want to read this whole incredible (and rather terrifying) story, I suggest Foundations, a book written by Rene A. Wormser who was general counsel to the Reece Committee. His book was published in 1958 by The Devin-Adair Company.

In the final report on Tax-Exempt Foundations, which the late Congressman Reece made for his ill-fated Special Committee (Report published December 16, 1954, by the Government Printing Office), Mr. Reece said:

"Miss Casey's report (Hearings pp. 877, et seq.) shows clearly the interlock between The Carnegie Endowment for International Peace, and some of its associated organizations, such as the Council on Foreign Relations and other foundations, with the State Department. Indeed, these foundations and organizations would not dream of denying this interlock. They proudly note it in reports. They have undertaken vital research projects for the Department; virtually created minor departments or groups within the Department for it; supplied advisors and executives from their ranks; fed a constant stream of personnel into the State Department trained by themselves or under programs which they have financed; and have had much to do with the formulation of foreign policy both in principle and detail.

"They have, to a marked degree, acted as direct agents of the State Department. And they have engaged actively, and with the expenditure of enormous sums, in propagandizing ('educating'?) public opinion in support of the policies which they have helped to formulate . . .

"What we see here is a number of large foundations, primarily The Rockefeller Foundation, The Carnegie Corporation of New York, and the Carnegie Endowment for International Peace, using their enormous public funds to finance a one-sided approach to foreign policy and to promote it actively, among the public by propaganda, and in the Government through infiltration. The power to do this comes out of the power of the vast funds employed."

Mr. Reece listed The Council on Foreign Relations, The Institute of International Education, The Foreign Policy Association, and The Institute of Pacific Relations, as among the interlocking organizations which are "agencies of these foundations," and pointed out that research and propaganda which does not support the "globalism" (or internationalism) to which all of these agencies are dedicated, receive little support from the tax-exempt foundations.

I disagree with Mr. Reece here, only in the placing of emphasis. As I see it, the foundations (which do finance the vast, complex, and powerful interlock of organizations devoted to a socialist one-world system) have, nonetheless, become the "agencies" of the principal organization which they finance—the Council on Foreign Relations.

* * * * *

The Reece Committee investigation threw some revealing light on the historical blackout which the Council on Foreign Relations has ordered and conducted.

Men who run the Council do not want the policies and measures of Franklin D. Roosevelt to undergo the critical analysis and objective study which exposed the policies of Woodrow Wilson after World War I. The Council has decided that the official propaganda of World War II must be perpetuated as history and the public protected from learning the truth. Hence, the Council sponsors historical works which give the socialist-internationalist version of historical events prior to and during World War II, while ignoring, or debunking, revisionist studies which attempt to tell the truth.

Here is how all of this is put in the 1946 Annual Report of the Rockefeller Foundation:

"The Committee on Studies of the Council on Foreign Relations is concerned that the debunking journalistic campaign following World War I should not be repeated and believes that the American public deserves a clear competent statement of our basic aims and activities during the second World War."

In 1946, the Rockefeller Foundation allotted $139,000 to the cost of a two-volume history of World War II, written by William L. Langer, a member of the CFR, and S. Everett Gleason. The generous grant was supplemented by a gift of $10,000 from the Alfred P. Sloan Foundation. The Langer-Gleason work was published by Harper and Brothers for the Council on Foreign Relations: Volume I in 1952 under the title, The Challenge To Isolationism, 1937-1940; Volume II in 1953, under the title, The Undeclared War.

The CFR's stated purpose in bringing out this work was to head off the revisionist historians like Charles Callan Tansill, Harry Elmer Barnes, Frederic R. Sanborn, George Morgenstern, Frances Neilson. The truth,

181

however, is not easy to suppress. Though written by and for the CFR, to perpetuate that organization's version of history, the Langer-Gleason volumes contain a wealth of information which helps to prove the basic thesis of this present volume.

* * * * *

One thing that the ill-fated Reece Committee found out in 1953-55, when trying to investigate the foundations, is that the tax-exempt organizations are set up, not for the purpose of doing some good in our society, but for the purpose of avoiding the income tax.

Rene A. Wormser, in Foundation says:

> "The chief motivation in the creation of foundations has long ceased to be pure philanthropy—it is now predominantly tax avoidance . . . The increasing tax burden on income and estates has greatly accelerated a trend toward creation of foundations as instruments for the retention of control over capital assets that would otherwise be lost . . .
>
> "The creation of a new foundation very often serves the purpose of contributing to a favorable public opinion for the person or corporation that endows it . . ."

The tax-exempt organizations have a vested interest in the oppressive, inequitable, and wasteful federal-income-tax system. Tax experts have devised, for example, a complicated scheme by which a wealthy man can actually save money by giving to tax-exempt organizations.

In short, many of the great philanthropies which buy fame and respectability for wealthy individuals, or corporations, are tax-avoidance schemes which, every year, add billions to the billions of private capital which is thus sterilized. These accumulations of tax-exempt billions place a heavier burden on taxpayers. Removing billions from taxation, the tax-exempt organizations thus obviously make taxpayers pay more in order to produce all that government demands.

* * * * *

The big tax-exempt organizations use their tax-exempt billions to buy prestige and power for themselves, and to bludgeon some critics into silence. For example, the Ford Foundation established the Fund for the Republic with a 15 million dollar grant in 1952–at a time when public awareness of the communist danger was seeping into the thinking of enough Americans to create a powerful anti-communist movement in this country.

By late 1955, the Fund's activities (publicly granting awards to fifth-amendment communists and so on) had become so blatant that public indignation was rising significantly. Just at the right time, the Ford Foundation announced a gift of 500 million dollars to the colleges of America.

Newspapers–also beholden in many ways to the big foundations–which will not publish news about the foundations' anti-American activities, give banner headlines to the lavish benefactions for purposes universally believed to be good.

Where will you find a college administration that will not defend the Ford Foundation against all critics–if the college has just received, or is in line to receive, a million-dollar gift from the Foundation?

How far must you search to find college professors or school teachers who will not defend the Foundation which gives 25 million dollars at one time, to raise the salaries of professors or school teachers?

Where will you find a plain John Doe citizen who is not favorably impressed that the hospitals and colleges in his community have received a multi-million dollar gift from a big foundation?

Every significant movement to destroy the American way of life has been directed and financed, in whole or in part, by tax-exempt organizations, which are entrenched in public opinion as benefactors of our society.

Worst of all: this tremendous power and prestige are in the hands of what Rene Wormser calls a special elite–a group of eggheads like Robert Hutchins (or worse) who neither understand nor respect the profit-motivated economic principles and the great political ideal of individual-freedom-under-limited-government which made our nation great.

Overlapping of personnel clearly shows a tight interlock between the Council on Foreign Relations and the big foundations.

The following information, concerning assets and officers of foundations, all comes from The Foundation Directory, prepared by The Foundation Library Center and published by the Russell Sage Foundation, New York City, 1960.

FORD FOUNDATION: Assets totaling $3,316,000,000.00 (3 billion, 316 million) on September 30, 1959. The Trustees of the Ford Foundation are: Eugene R. Black (CFR); James B. Black; James F. Brownlee; John Cowles (CFR); Donald K. David (CFR); Mark F. Ethridge (CFR); Benson Ford; Henry Ford II; H. Rowan Gaither, Jr. (CFR); Laurence M. Gould (CFR); Henry T. Heald (CFR); Roy E. Larsen; John J. McCloy (CFR); Julius A. Stratton (CFR); Charles E. Wyzanski, Jr. (CFR).

Note that of the 15 members of the Board of Trustees, 10 are members of the Council on Foreign Relations (CFR).

FUND FOR THE REPUBLIC, Santa Barbara, California, a subsidiary of Ford, had assets totaling $6,667,022.00 on September 30, 1957. Officers and directors: Robert Hutchins; Paul G. Hoffman (CFR); Elmo Roper (CFR); George N. Shuster (CFR); Harry S. Ashmore; Bruce Catton; Charles W. Cole (CFR); Arthur J. Goldberg; William H. Joyce, Jr.; Meyer Kestnbaum (CFR); Msgr. Francis Lally; Herbert H. Lehman (CFR); M.

Albert Linton; J. Howard Marshall; Jubal R. Parten; Alicia Patterson; Mrs. Eleanor B. Stevenson; Henry P. Van Dusen (CFR).

Note that 7 of the 18 are CFR members.

ROCKEFELLER FOUNDATION, 111 West 50th Street, New York 20, New York, had assets totaling $647,694,858.00 on December 31, 1958. Officers and Trustees: John D. Rockefeller 3rd (CFR); Dean Rusk (CFR); Barry Bingham; Chester Bowles (CFR); Lloyd D. Brace; Richard Bradfield (CFR); Detlev W. Bronk (CFR); Ralph J. Bunche (CFR); John S. Dickey (CFR); Lewis W. Douglas (CFR); Lee A. DuBridge; Wallace K. Harrison; Arthur A. Houghton, Jr. (CFR); John R. Kimberly (CFR); Robert F. Loeb; Robert A. Lovett (CFR); Benjamin M. McKelway; Henry Allen Moe; Henry P. Van Dusen (CFR); W. Barry Wood, Jr.

Of the 20, 12 are CFR members.

ROCKEFELLER BROTHERS FUND, 30 Rockefeller Plaza, New York 20, New York, had assets totaling $53,174,210.00 on December 31, 1958. Officers and Trustees: Laurence S. Rockefeller; David Rockefeller (CFR); Detlev W. Bronk (CFR); Wallace K. Harrison; Abby Rockefeller Mauze; Abby M. O'Neill; John D. Rockefeller 3rd (CFR); Nelson A. Rockefeller (CFR); Winthrop Rockefeller.

Of the 9, 4 are CFR members.

CARNEGIE CORPORATION OF NEW YORK, 589 Fifth Avenue, New York 17, New York, had assets totaling $261,244,471.00 on September 30, 1959. Officers and Trustees: John W. Gardner (CFR); Morris Hadley; James A. Perkins (CFR); Robert F. Bacher; Caryl P. Haskins (CFR); C. D. Jackson (CFR); Devereux C. Josephs (CFR); Nicholas Kelley (CFR); Malcolm A. MacIntyre (CFR); Margaret Carnegie Miller; Frederick Osborn (CFR); Gwilym A. Price; Elihu

Root, Jr. (CFR); Frederick Sheffield; Charles Spofford (CFR); Charles Allen Thomas.

Of the 16, 10 are CFR members.

CARNEGIE ENDOWMENT FOR INTERNATIONAL PEACE, United Nations Plaza & 46th Street, New York 17, New York, had a net worth of $22,577,134.00 on June 30, 1958. Officers and Trustees: Joseph E. Johnson (CFR); Whitney North Seymour (CFR); O. Frederick Nolde; Lawrence S. Finkelstein (CFR); Arthur K. Watson (CFR); James M. Nicely (CFR); Dillon Anderson (CFR); Charles E. Beard; Robert Blum (CFR); Harvey H. Bundy (CFR); David L. Cole; Frederick S. Dunn (CFR); Arthur J. Goldberg; Ernest A. Gross (CFR); Philip C. Jessup (CFR); Milton Katz (CFR); Grayson L. Kirk (CFR); Mrs. Clare Boothe Luce; Charles A. Meyer (CFR); Otto L. Nelson, Jr.; Ellmore C. Patterson (CFR); Howard C. Petersen (CFR); Howard P. Robertson; David Rockefeller (CFR); W. J. Schieffelin, Jr.; George N. Shuster (CFR).

Of the 26, 18 are CFR members.

CARNEGIE FOUNDATION FOR THE ADVANCEMENT OF TEACHING, had assets totaling $20,043,859.00 on June 30, 1959. Officers and Trustees: Carter Davidson (CFR); John W. Gardner (CFR); James A. Perkins (CFR); William F. Houston; Harvie Branscomb; Arthur H. Dean (CFR); Robert F. Goheen (CFR); Laurence M. Gould (CFR); A. Whitney Griswold (CFR); Rufus C. Harris; Frederick L. Hovde (CFR); Clark Kerr; Lawrence A. Kimpton; Grayson L. Kirk (CFR); Thomas S. Lamont (CFR); Robert A. Lovett (CFR); Howard F. Lowry; N. A. M. MacKenzie; Katharine E. McBride; Millicent C. McIntosh; John S. Millis (CFR); Franklin D. Murphy (CFR); Nathan M. Pusey (CFR); Herman B. Wells (CFR); Logan Wilson; O. Meredith Wilson.

Of the 26, 15 are CFR members.

186

CARNEGIE INSTITUTE OF WASHINGTON, 1530 "P" Street, N.W., Washington 5, D. C., had assets totaling $80,838,528.00 on June 30, 1958. Officers and Trustees: Caryl P. Haskins (CFR); Walter S. Gifford (CFR); Barklie McKee Henry; Robert Woods Bliss (CFR); James F. Bell; General Omar N. Bradley; Vannevar Bush; Crawford H. Greenewalt; Alfred L. Loomis (CFR); Robert A. Lovett (CFR); Keith S. McHugh; Margaret Carnegie Miller; Henry S. Morgan (CFR); Seeley G. Mudd; William I. Myers; Henning W. Prentis, Jr.; Elihu Root, Jr. (CFR); Henry R. Shepley; Charles P. Taft; Juan Terry Trippe (CFR); James N. White; Robert E. Wilson.

Of the 22, 8 are CFR members.

ALFRED P. SLOAN FOUNDATION, 630 Fifth Avenue, New York 20, New York, had assets totaling $175,533,110.00 on December 31, 1958. Officers and Trustees: Albert Bradley (CFR); Alfred P. Sloan, Jr. (CFR); Raymond P. Sloan; Arnold J. Zurcher (CFR); Frank W. Abrams; Henry C. Alexander (CFR); Walter S. Carpenter, Jr. (CFR); General Lucius D. Clay (CFR); John L. Collyer (CFR); Lewis W. Douglas (CFR); Frank A. Howard; Devereux C. Josephs (CFR); Mervin J. Kelly (CFR); James R. Killian, Jr. (CFR); Laurence S. Rockefeller; George Whitney (CFR).

Of the 16, 12 are CFR members.

THE COMMONWEALTH FUND OF NEW YORK, 5500 Maspeth Avenue, New York 78, New York, had assets totaling $119,904,614.00 on June 30, 1959. Officers and Trustees: Malcolm P. Aldrich; John A. Gifford; Leo D. Welch (CFR); George P. Berry; Roger M. Blough (CFR); Harry P. Davison (CFR); Harold B. Hoskins; J. Quigg Newton (CFR); William E. Stevenson (CFR); Henry C. Taylor.

Of the 10, 6 are CFR members.

TWENTIETH CENTURY FUND, INC., 41 East 70th Street, New York 3, New York, had assets totaling $17,522,441.00 on December 31, 1958. Officers and Trustees: Adolf A. Berle, Jr. (CFR); Francis Biddle (CFR); August Heckscher (CFR); Hans Christian Sonne (CFR); Morris B. Abram; Arthur F. Burns (CFR); Erwin D. Canham (CFR); Evans Clark (CFR); Benjamin V. Cohen (CFR); Wallace K. Harrison (CFR); David E. Lilienthal (CFR); Robert S. Lynd; James G. McDonald (CFR); J. Robert Oppenheimer (CFR); Edmund Orgill; James H. Rowe, Jr.; Arthur M. Schlesinger, Jr. (CFR); Herman W. Steinkraus; Charles P. Taft; W. W. Waymack.

Of the 20, 13 are CFR members.

CHAPTER 12.

WHY? WHAT CAN WE DO?

Claiming to believe in the high destiny of America as a world-leader, our invisible government urges timid policies of appeasement and surrender which make America a world whipping-boy rather than a world leader. Claiming to believe in the dignity and worth of the human individual, the modern liberals who run our invisible government urge an ever-growing welfare-state which is destroying individualism—which has already so weakened the American sense of personal responsibility that crime rates have increased 98 percent in our land during the past ten years.

Why? Why do prominent Americans support programs which are so harmful? It is a difficult question to answer.

* * * * *

Somewhere at the top of the pyramid in the invisible government are a few sinister people who know exactly what they are doing: they want America to become part of a worldwide socialist dictatorship, under the control of the Kremlin.

* * * * *

Some may actually dislike communists, but feel that one-world socialism is desirable and inevitable. They are working with a sense of urgency for a "benign" world socialist dictatorship to forestall the Kremlin from imposing its brand of world dictatorship by force.

* * * * *

Some leaders in the invisible government are brilliant and power-hungry men who feel that the masses are unable to govern themselves and who want to set up a great dictatorship which will give them power to arrange things for the masses.

The leadership of the invisible government doubtless rests in the hands of a sinister or power-hungry few; but its real strength is in the thousands of Americans who have been drawn into the web for other reasons. Many, if not most, of these are status-seekers.

* * * * *

When you are a rising junior executive, or a man of any age looking for good business and social connections, it seems good to go to a luncheon where you can sit at the head table and call leaders of the community by their first names. Most of the propaganda agencies affiliated with the Council on Foreign Relations provide such opportunities for members.

A businessman enjoys coming home from a black-tie affair in New York or Washington where he and a few other "chosen" men have been given a "confidential, off-the-record briefing" by some high governmental official. The Council on Foreign Relations provides such experiences for officials of companies which contribute money to the CFR.

This status-seeking is a way of life for thousands of American businessmen. Some of them would not give it up even if they knew their activities were supporting the socialist revolution, although at heart they are opposed to socialism. Most of them, however, would withdraw from the Foreign Policy Association, and the World Affairs Councils, and the Committee for Economic Development, and the American Association for the UN, and the National Conference of Christians and Jews, and the

190

Advertising Council, and similar organizations, if they were educated to an understanding of what their membership in such organizations really means.

The job of every American who knows and cares is to make sure that all of the people in the invisible government network know exactly what they are doing.

* * * * *

But beyond that, what can we do? What can we Americans do about the Council on Foreign Relations and its countless tentacles of power and money and influence and propaganda which are wrapped around all the levers of political power in Washington; which reach into the schools and churches and respected civic organizations of America; which control major media of communications; which are insinuated into controlling positions in the big unions; and which even have a grip on the prestige and money of major American corporations?

It is often suggested that investigation by the FBI might be the answer.

For example, after the March-April Term (1960) Grand Jury in Fulton County, Georgia, condemned Foreign Policy Association literature as "insidious and subversive" and the American Legion Post published The Truth About The Foreign Policy Association to document the Grand Jury's findings (see Chapter V), supporters of the Foreign Policy Association denounced the legionnaires, saying, in effect, that if there were a need to investigate the FPA, the investigation should be done in proper, legal manner by trained FBI professionals and not by "vigilantes" and "amateurs" and "bigoted ignoramuses" on some committee of an American Legion Post.

This is an effective propaganda technique. It gives many the idea that the organization under criticism has nothing to hide and is willing to have

191

all its activities thoroughly investigated, if the investigation is conducted properly and decently.

* * * * *

But the fact is that the FBI has no jurisdiction to investigate the kind of activities engaged in by the Foreign Policy Association and its related and affiliated organizations. The Foreign Policy Association is not a communist organization. If it were, it could be handled easily. The Attorney General and the committees of Congress could simply post it as a communist organization. Then, it would receive support only from people who are conscious instruments of the communist conspiracy; and there are not, relatively, very many of those in the United States.

The FPA's Councils on World Affairs are supported by patriotic community leaders. Yet, these Councils have done more than all communists have ever managed to do, in brainwashing the American people with propaganda for governmental intervention in the economic affairs of the people, and for endless permanent entanglement in the affairs of foreign nations—thus preparing this nation for submergence in a one-world socialist system, which is the objective of communism.

* * * * *

Inasmuch as the invisible government is composed of organizations which enjoy the special privilege of federal tax-exemption (a privilege seldom given to organizations advocating return to traditional American policies) it is often suggested that public pressures might persuade the Treasury Department to withdraw the tax-exempt privilege from these organizations.

How could the Treasury Department ever be persuaded to take action against the Council on Foreign Relations, when the Council controls the Department? Douglas Dillon, Secretary of the Treasury, is a member of the CFR.

192

It is impractical to think of getting Treasury Department action against the CFR. Moreover, such a solution to the problem could be dangerous.

A governmental agency which has limitless power to withdraw special tax-privileges must also have limitless power to grant special privileges. The Treasury Department could destroy all of the organizations composing the invisible government interlock by the simple action of withdrawing the tax-exempt privilege, thus drying up major sources of revenue. But the Treasury Department could then create another Frankenstein monster by giving tax-exemption to other organizations.

It is often suggested that some congressional committee investigate the Council on Foreign Relations and the network of organizations interlocked with it.

Yet, as we have seen, two different committees of Congress—one Democrat-controlled and one Republican-controlled—have tried to investigate the big tax-exempt foundations which are interlocked with, and controlled by, and provide the primary source of revenue for, the Council on Foreign Relations and its affiliates.

Both committees were gutted with ridicule and vicious denunciation, not just by the official communist party press, but by internationalists in the Congress, by spokesmen for the executive branch of government, and by big respected publishing and broadcasting firms which are a part of the controlled propaganda network of the Council on Foreign Relations.

* * * * *

The invisible government is not, however, beyond the reach of the whole Congress, if the Congress has the spur and support of an informed public.

Our only hope lies in the Congress which is responsive to public will, when that will is fully and insistently expressed.

Every time I suggest that aroused citizens write their Congressmen and Senators, I get complaints from people who say they have been writing for years and that it does no good.

Yet, remember the Connally Reservation issue in January, 1960. The Humphrey Resolution (to repeal the Connally Reservation and thus permit the World Court to assume unlimited jurisdiction over American affairs) was before the Senate Foreign Relations Committee. The Chairman of this Committee was J. William Fulbright (Democrat, Arkansas) a Rhodes-scholar internationalist, determined to repeal the Connally Reservation. Leaders in Congress and in the Administration were determined to repeal the Connally Reservation, and so was the invisible government of the United States–which means that the vast thought-controlling machine of the CFR (radio and television networks; major newspapers and magazines; and an imposing array of civic, church, professional, and "educational" organizations) had been in high gear for many months, saturating the public with "world-peace-through-world-law" propaganda intended to shame and scare the public into accepting repeal of the Connally Reservation.

But word got out, and the American public positively Stunned Congress with protests. Fulbright let the resolution die in committee.

The expression of public will was massive and explosive in connection with the Connally Reservation, whereas in connection with many other equally important issues, the public seems indifferent. The reason is that the Connally Reservation is a simple issue. It is easy for a voter to write or wire his elected representatives saying, "Let's keep the Connally Reservation"; or, "If you vote for repeal of the Connally Reservation, I'll vote against you."

What kind of wire or letter can a voter send his elected representatives concerning the bigger and more important issue which I have labeled "Invisible Government"?

The ultimate solution lies in many sweeping and profound changes in the policies of government, which cannot be effected until a great many

194

more Americans have learned a great deal more about the American constitutional system than they know now.

* * * * *

But there is certain action which the people could demand of Congress immediately; and every Congressman and Senator who refuses to support such action could be voted out of office the next time he stands for re-election.

1. We should demand that Congress amend the Internal Revenue Code in such a way that no agency of the executive branch of government will have the power to grant federal tax-exemption. The Constitution gives the power of taxation only to the Congress. Hence, only Congress should have the power to grant exemption from taxation.

Instead of permitting the Internal Revenue Service of the Treasury Department to decide whether a foundation or any other organization shall have federal tax-exemption, Congress should exercise this power, fully publicizing and frequently reviewing all grants of tax-exemption.

2. In addition to demanding that Congress take the power of granting and withholding federal tax-exemption away from the executive agencies, voters should demand that the House of Representatives form a special committee to investigate the Council on Foreign Relations and its associated foundations and other organizations.

The investigation should be conducted for the same purpose that the great McCarran investigation of the Institute of Pacific Relations was conducted—that is, to identify the people and organizations involved

195

and to provide an authentic record, of the invisible government's aims and programs, and personnel, for the public to see and study. Such an investigation, if properly conducted, would thoroughly discredit the invisible government in the eyes of the American people.

* * * * *

There is, however, only one sure and final way to stop this great and growing evil—and that is to cut it out as if it were cancerous, which it is. The only way to cut it out is to eliminate the income-tax system which spawned it.

The federal income-tax system suckles the forces which are destroying our free and independent republic. Abolish the system, and the sucklings will die of starvation.

That is the ultimate remedy, but before we can compel Congress to provide this remedy, we must have an educated electorate. The problem of educating the public is great—not because of the inability of the people to understand, but because of the difficulty of reaching them with the freedom story.

If the federal government, during the 1962 fiscal year, had not collected one penny in tax on personal incomes, the government would still have had more tax revenue from other sources than the total of what Harry Truman collected in his most extravagant peacetime spending year. Every American, who knows that, can readily understand the possibility and the necessity of repealing the federal tax on personal incomes. But how many Americans know those simple facts? The job of everyone who knows and cares is to get such facts to others.

* * * * *

Even if we did take action to divest the Council on Foreign Relations and its powerful interlock of control over our government; and even if we did reverse the policies which are now dragging us into a one-world socialist dictatorship–what would we do about some of the dangerous messes which our policies already have us involved in? What, for example, could we do about Cuba? About Berlin?

In some ways, the policies of our invisible government have taken us beyond the point of no return. Consider the problem of Cuba. Armed intervention in the affairs of another nation violates the principles of the traditional American policy of benign neutrality, to which I think our nation should return. Yet, our intervention in Cuban affairs (on the side of communism) has produced such a dangerous condition that we should now intervene with armed might in the interest of our own survival.

* * * * *

For sixteen years, we have seen the disastrous fallacy of trying to handle the foreign affairs of our great nation through international agencies. This leaves us without a policy of our own, and makes it impossible for us to take any action in our own interest or against the interests of communism, because communists have more actual votes, and infinitely more influence, in all the international agencies than we have. At the same time, our enemies, the communist nations, set and follow their own policies, contemptuously ignoring the international agencies which hamstring America and bleed American taxpayers for subsidies to our mortal enemies.

America must do two things soon if she expects to survive as a free and independent nation:

(1) We must withdraw from membership in all international, governmental, or quasi-governmental, organizations–including, specifically, the World Court, the United Nations, and all UN specialized agencies. (2) We must act vigorously, unilaterally, and quickly, to protect vital American security interests in the Western Hemisphere–particularly in Cuba.

We have already passed the time when we can act in Cuba easily and at no risk; but if we have any sane, manly concern for protecting the vital security of the American nation and the lives and property of United States citizens, we had better do the only thing left for us to do: send overwhelming American military force to take Cuba over quickly, and keep it under American military occupation, as beneficently as possible, until the Cuban people can hold free elections to select their own government.

The other nations of the world would scream; but they would, nonetheless, respect us. Such action in our own interests is the only thing that will restore our "prestige" in the world–and restore American military security in the Western Hemisphere.

* * * * *

What should we do about Berlin?

The Berlin problem must be solved soon, because it is too effectively serving the purpose for which it was created in the first place: to justify whatever programs the various governments involved want to pursue.

It sometimes looks as if the Kremlin and Washington officialdom are working hand-in-glove to deceive the people of both nations, turning the Berlin "crisis" on and off to cover up failures and to provide excuses for more adventures.

Berlin will cause a world war only when the United States is willing to go to war with the Soviet Union to free Berlin from the trap it is in. If we won't defend our own vital interests against the aggressive and arrogant actions of communists 90 miles from our shores, what would prompt us to cross the ocean and defend Germans from communists?

The cold fact of the matter is that we should not defend Berlin. This is a job for Germans, not Americans.

The Germans are an able and prosperous people. They are capable of fighting their own war, if war is necessary to protect them from communism.

It is inaccurate to refer to the eastern part of Germany as "communist Germany." That part of Germany is under communist enslavement; but the Germans who live there probably hate communists more than any other people on earth do.

The uprisings of 1953, and the endless stream of refugees fleeing from the communist zone in Germany, are proof enough that the communists could not hold East Germany without the presence of Soviet troops.

There is enough hunger and poverty and hatred of communism in eastern Germany to justify the conclusion that even Khrushchev knows he has a bear by the tail there. If we would do our part, Khrushchev would either turn loose and run; or the bear would pull loose and destroy Khrushchev.

What part should we play? We should do exactly what the President and the State Department assure the world they will not do: we should present the Soviets with a fait accompli, and an ultimatum.

We should call an immediate conference with the governments of France, England, and West Germany to explain that America has devoted 16 years and many billions of dollars to rehabilitating and defending western Europe; that Europe is now in many ways more soundly prosperous than we are; that the 180 million Americans can no longer be expected to ruin their own economy and neglect the defense of their own homeland for the purpose of assisting and defending the 225 million people of Western Europe; and that, therefore, we are through.

We have no need, at home, for all of the vast stores of military equipment which we now have in Europe for the defense of Europe. What we do not need for the defense of our homeland, we should offer as a gift to West Germany, since we produced the material in the first place for the purpose of resisting communism, and since the West Germans are the only people in Western Europe who apparently want to resist it.

We should give the West Germans (and the other western powers) six months to train whatever manpower they want for manning their own defenses. At the end of that time, we should pull out and devote ourselves to defending America.

With or without the consent of France and England, we should sign a peace treaty with the government of Western Germany, recognizing it as the lawful government of all Germany and imposing no restrictions on the sovereignty of Germany—that is, leaving Germany free to arm as it pleases.

Immediately following the signing of this treaty, we should announce to the world that, when we pull out of Europe at the end of six months, we expect the Soviets to pull out of Germany entirely. If, within one week after we effect our withdrawal, the Soviets are not out—or if they later come back in, against the wishes of the German nation—we should break off diplomatic relations with all communist countries; deny all representatives of all communist nations access to United Nations headquarters which are on United States soil; and exert maximum pressures throughout the world to isolate all communist countries, economically and diplomatically, from all non-communist countries.

That is an American plan, which would solve the German "problem" in the interests of peace and freedom.

* * * * *

Many Americans, who see what the solution to our grave problems ought to be, have lost hope that we will ever achieve such solution, because, in the end, the solution rests with the people.

It is the people who must compel their elected representatives to make a thorough investigation of the Council on Foreign Relations and its interlock.

It is the people who must compel Congress to deny administrative Agencies of government the unconstitutional power of granting tax-exemption.

It is the people who must compel Congress to submit a constitutional amendment calling for repeal of the income tax amendment.

It is the people who must compel Washington officialdom to do what is right and best for America in foreign affairs, especially in Cuba and Berlin.

Many Americans are in despair because they feel that the people will never do these things. These pessimists seem to share the late Harry Hopkins' conviction that the American people are too dumb to think.

I do not believe it. I subscribe to the marvelous doctrine of Thomas Jefferson, who said:

> "I know no safe depository of the ultimate powers of society but the people themselves; and if we think them not enlightened enough to exercise their control with a wholesome discretion, the remedy is not to take it from them, but to inform their discretion by education."

APPENDIX I.

COUNCIL ON FOREIGN RELATIONS MEMBERSHIP ROSTER

This roster of membership is from the 1960-61 Annual Report of the CFR.

Directors

Frank Altschul 1984-
Hamilton Fish Armstrong 1928-
Elliott V. Bell 1953-
Isaiah Bowman 1921-1950
William A. M. Burden 1945-
Archibald Cary Coolidge 1921-1928
Paul D. Cravath 1921-1940
John W. Davis 1921-1955
Norman H. Davis 1921-1944
Arthur H. Dean 1955-
Harold W. Dodds 1935-1943
Lewis W. Douglas 1940-
Stephen P. Duggan 1921-1950
Allen W. Dulles 1927-
Thomas K. Finletter 1944-
John H. Finley 1921-1929
William C. Foster 1959-
Leon Fraser 1936-1945

Edwin F. Gay 1921-1945
W. Averell Harrman 1950-1955
Caryl P. Haskins 1961-
David F. Houston 1921-1927
Charles P. Howland 1929-1931
Clarence E. Hunter 1942-1953
Philip C. Jessup 1934-1942
Joseph E. Johnson 1950-
Devereux C. Josephs 1951-1958
Otto H. Kahn 1921-1934
Grayson L. Kirk 1950-
R. C. Leffingwell 1927-1960
Walter Lippman 1932-1937
Walter H. Mallory 1945, 1951-
George O. May 1927-1953
John J. McCloy 1953-
Wesley C. Mitchell 1927-1934
Frank L. Polk 1921-1943
Philip D. Reed 1945-
Winfield W. Riefler 1945-1950
David Rockefeller 1949-
Whitney H. Shepardson 1921-
William R. Shepherd 1921-1927
Charles M. Spofford 1955-
Adlai E. Stevenson 1958-
Myron C. Taylor 1943-1959
Paul M. Warburg 1921-1932
Edward Warner 1940-1945
George W. Wickersham 1921-1936
John H. Williams 1937-
Clarence M. Woolley 1932-1935

Henry M. Wriston 1943-
Owen D. Young 1927-1940

Resident Members

Albrecht-Carrie, Rene
Aldrich, Winthrop W.
Alexander, Archibald S.
Alexander, Henry C.
Alexander, Robert J.
Allan, F. Aley
Allen, Charles E.
Allen, Philip E.
Alley, James B.
Allport, Alexander W.
Alpern, Alan N.
Altschul, Arthur G.
Altschul, Frank
Ames, Amyas
Ammidon, Hoyt
Anderson, Arthur M.
Anderson, Harold F.
Anderson, Robert B.
Angell, James W.
Armour, Norman
Armstrong, Hamilton Fish
Ascoli, Max
Aubrey, Henry G.
Ault, Bromwell

Backer, George
Baker, Edgar R.

Baldwin, Hanson W.
Bancroft, Harding F.
Barber, Charles F.
Barber, Joseph
Barker, Robert R.
Barkin, Solomon
Barnes, Joseph
Barnett, A. Doak
Barnett, Frank R.
Barrett, Edward W.
Bastedo, Philip
Baumer, William H.
Baxter, James P., 3rd
Beal, Gerald F.
Beckhart, Benjamin H.
Bedard, Pierre
Beebe, Frederick S.
Bell, Elliott V.
Bennett, John C.
Benton, William B.
Beplat, Tristan E.
Berle, Adolf A., Jr.
Bessie, Simon Michael
Bevis, Herman W.
Bidwell, Percy W.
Bienstock, Abraham L.
Bingham, Jonathan B.
Black, Peter
Blair, Floyd G.
Blake, Robert O.
Blough, Roger M.
Blough, Roy

Blum, John A.
Boardman, Arthur G., Jr.
Bogdan, Norbert A.
Bolte, Charles G.
Bonsal, Dudley B.
Boorman, Howard L.
Boyd, Hugh N.
Braden, Spruille
Bradford, Amory H.
Bramstedt, W. F.
Braxton, Carter M.
Breck, Henry C.
Brinckeroff, Charles M.
Brittenham, Raymond L.
Bronk, Detlev W.
Brown, Courtney C.
Brown, Francis
Brown, John Mason
Brown, Walter L.
Brownell, George A.
Brownell, Lincoln C.
Bruce, James
Brzezinski, Zbigniew
Bullock, Hugh
Bunche, Ralph J.
Bunker, Arthur H.
Bunker, Ellsworth
Bunnell, C. Sterling
Burden, William A. M.
Burgess, Carter L.
Burkhardt, Frederick
Burns, Arthur F.

Bush, Donald F.
Butler, William F.
Buttenwieser, Benjamin J.

Cain, Charles, Jr.
Calder, Alexander, Jr.
Calhoun, Alexander D.
Campbell, H. Donald
Campbell, John C.
Canfield, Cass
Carey, Andrew G.
Carpenter, George W.
Carroll, Mitchell B.
Carson, Ralph M.
Case, James H., Jr.
Case, John C.
Cattier, Jean
Chadbourne, William M.
Champion, George
Chase, W. Howard
Cheney, Ward
Childs, Thomas W.
Christie, Lansdell K.
Chubb, Percy, 2nd
Church, Edgar M.
Clapp, Gordon R.
Clark, Brig. Gen. Edwin N.
Clark, James F.
Clay, Gen. Lucius D.
Clinchy, Everett R.
Coffin, Edmund
Cohen, Jerome B.

Collado, Emilio G.
Collings, L. V.
Collingwood, Charles P.
Colwell, Kent G.
Conant, James B.
Conant, Melvin
Cook, Howard A.
Coombs, Charles A.
Cooper, Franklin S.
Cordier, Andrew W.
Cousins, Norman
Cowan, L. Gray
Cowles, Gardner
Cox, Charles R.
Creel, Dana S.
Cummings, Robert L., Jr.
Cusick, Peter

Dallin, Alexander
Danner, Arthur V.
Darrell, Norris
Daum, Earl C.
Davenport, John
Davis, Norman P.
Davison, W. Phillips
Dean, Arthur H.
Debevoise, Eli Whitney
De Lima, Oscar A.
De Vegh, Imrie
De Vries, Henry P.
Dewey, Thomas E.
D'Harnoncourt, Rene

Diebold, William, Jr.
Dillon, Clarence
Dilworth, J. Richardson
Dodge, Cleveland E.
Donner, Frederick G.
Donovan, Hedley
Dorr, Goldthwaite H.
Dorwin, Oscar John
Douglas, Lewis W.
Douglas, Percy L.
Dryfoos, Orvil E.
Dubinsky, David
DuBois, J. Delafield
Durdin, Tillman

Eagle, Vernon A.
Eaton, Fredrick M.
Eberstadt, Ferdinand
Edelman, Albert I.
Eder, Phanor J.
Eichelberger, Clark M.
Elliott, L. W.
Emmet, Christopher
Engel, Irving M.
Ernst, Albert E.
Erpf, Armand G.
Evans, Roger F.
Eveleth, George S., Jr.
Ewing, Sherman
Ewing, William, Jr.
Exter, John

Fahs, Charles B.
Field, William Osgood, Jr.
Fischer, John S.
Fisher, Henry J.
Fleck, G. Peter
Fleischmann, Manly
Florinsky, Michael T.
Ford, Nevil
Forkner, Claude E.
Forrestal, Michael V.
Fosdick, Raymond B.
Fox, Joseph C.
Fox, William T. R.
Foye, Arthur B.
Franklin, George S., Jr.
Franklin, John M.
Freedman, Emanuel R.
French, John
Freudenthal, David M.
Friele, Berent
Friendly, Henry J.
Fry, Varian
Fuerbringer, Otto
Fuller, C. Dale
Fuller, Robert G.

Galantiere, Lewis
Gallatin, James P.
Gamble, Sidney D.
Gant, George F.
Gardner, John W.
Garretson, Albert H.

Garrison, Lloyd K.
Gaston, George A.
Gates, Samuel E.
Gates, Thomas S.
Gay, Edward R.
Geneen, Harold S.
Gevers, Max E.
Gibney, Frank B.
Gideonse, Harry D.
Gifford, Walter S.
Gillespie, S. Hazard, Jr.
Gilpatric, Chadbourne
Golden, William T.
Goldsmith, Arthur
Goldstone, Harmon H.
Goodrich, Leland M.
Gordon, Albert H.
Goss, James H.
Grace, J. P., Jr.
Graff, Robert D.
Gray, William Latimer
Gray, William Steele
Grazier, Joseph A.
Griffith, Thomas
Grimm, Peter
Grondahl, Teg C.
Gross, Ernest A.
Grover, Allen
Guggenheim, Harry F.
Gunther, John
Gurfein, Murray I.

Haight, George W.
Hall, Perry E.
Hamilton, Thomas J.
Hamlin, Chauncey J.
Hammond, Capt. Paul
Hance, William A.
Hanes, John W., Jr.
Harrar, J. G.
Harriman, E. Roland
Hasler, Frederick E.
Hauge, Gabriel
Hayes, Alfred
Hazard, John N.
Heald, Henry T.
Heckscher, August
Heineman, Dannie N.
Henderson, William
Herod, W. Rogers
Herring, Pendleton
Herzog, Paul M.
Hess, Jerome S.
Hill, Forrest F.
Hill, James T. Jr.
Hill, John A.
Hills, Robert C.
Hirschman, Albert O.
Hochschild, Harold K.
Hochschild, Walter
Hoglund, Elis S.
Hoguet, Robert L., Jr.
Hohenberg, John
Holland, Henry F.

Holland, Kenneth
Holman, Eugene
Holst, Willem
Holt, L. Emmett, Jr.
Homer, Sidney, Jr.
Hoopes, Townsend
Hoover, Lyman
Horn, Garfield H.
Horton, Philip
Hottelet, Richard C.
Houghton, Arthur A., Jr.
Houston, Frank K.
Howard, John B.
Howe, John
Hughes, Emmet John
Hughes, John Chambers
Humphreys, H. E., Jr.
Hupper, Roscoe H.
Hurewitz, J. C.
Hyde, Henry B.
Hyde, James N.

Ide, John J.
Inglis, John B.
Irwin, John N., 2nd
Iselin, O'Donnell

Jackson, C. D.
Jackson, William E.
James, George F.
Jaretzki, Alfred, Jr.
Jay, Nelson Dean

Jessup, Alpheus W.
Jessup, John K.
Johnson, Edward F.
Johnson, Howard C.
Johnson, Joseph E.
Jones, David J.
Jones, W. Alton
Josephs, Devereux C.
Joubert, Richard Cheney

Kaminer, Peter H.
Kane, R. Keith
Kappel, Frederick E.
Keezer, Dexter Merriam
Keiser, David M.
Kelley, Nicholas
Kenney, F. Donald
Kern, Harry F.
Kettaneh, Francis A.
Keyser, Paul V., Jr.
Kiaer, Herman S.
King, Frederic R.
Kirk, Adm. Alan G.
Kirk, Grayson L.
Klots, Allen T.
Knoke, L. Werner
Knoppers, Antonie T.
Knowles, John Ellis
Knox, William E.
Koenig, Robert P.
Kohn, Hans
Kraft, Joseph

Lada-Mocarski, V.
La Farge, Francis W.
Lamb, Horace R.
Lamont, Peter T.
Lamont, Thomas S.
Lang, Robert E.
Larmon, Sigurd S.
LaRoche, Chester J.
Laukhuff, Perry
LeBaron, Eugene
Lee, Elliott H.
Lehman, Herbert H.
Lehman, Orin
Lehman, Robert
Lehrman, Hal
Leich, John F.
Leonard, James G.
Leroy, Norbert G.
Leslie, John C.
Levy, Walter J.
Lewis, Roger
Lewisohn, Frank
Lieberman, Henry R.
Lightner, M. C.
Lilienthal, David E.
Lindquist, Warren T.
Lissitzyn, Oliver J.
Lockwood, John E.
Lockwood, Mancie deF., 3rd
Lockwood, William A.
Lodge, Henry Cabot
Loeb, John L.

Logan, Sheridan A.
Loomis, Alfred L.
Loos, Rev. A. William
Loucks, Harold H.
Lounsbury, Robert H.
Lubin, Isador
Luce, Henry R.
Ludt, R. E.
Luitweiler, J. C.
Lunning, Just
Lyford, Joseph P.

McCance, Thomas
McCarthy, John G.
McCloy, John J.
McDaniel, Joseph M., Jr.
McDonald, James G.
McGraw, James H., Jr.
McKeever, Porter
McLean, Donald H., Jr.
MacDuffie, Marshall
MacEachron, David W.
MacIntyre, Malcolm A.
MacIver, Murdoch
MacVeagh, Ewen Cameron
Maffry, August
Maguire, Walter N.
Malin, Patrick Murphy
Mallory, Walter H.
Mark, Rev. Julius
Markel, Lester
Martino, Joseph A.

Marvel, William W.
Masten, John E.
Mathews, Edward J.
Mattison, Graham D.
May, A. Wilfred
May, Stacy
Menke, John R.
Merz, Charles
Metzger, Herman A.
Mickelson, Sig
Midtbo, Harold
Millar, D. G.
Millard, Mark J.
Miller, Edward G., Jr.
Miller, Paul R., Jr.
Miller, William J.
Millis, Walter
Mills, Bradford
Minor, Clark H.
Mitchell, Don G.
Mitchell, Sidney A.
Model, Leo
Monaghan, Thomas E.
Moore, Ben T.
Moore, Edward F.
Moore, George S.
Moore, Maurice T.
Moore, William T.
Morgan, Cecil
Morgan, D. P.
Morgan, Henry S.
Morris, Grinnell

Mosely, Philip E.
Muir, Malcolm
Munroe, Vernon, Jr.
Munyan, Winthrop R.
Murdin, Forrest D.
Murphy, Grayson M-P.
Murphy, J. Morden

Nason, John W.
Neal, Alfred C.
Nebolsine, George
Nicely, James M.
Nichols, Thomas S.
Nichols, William I.
Nickerson, A. L.
Nielsen, Waldemar A.
Nolte, Richard H.
Northrop, Johnston F.
Notestein, Frank W.
Noyes, Charles Phelps

Oakes, John B.
O'Brien, Justin
O'Connor, Roderic L.
Ogden, Alfred
Olds, Irving Sands
Oppenheimer, Fritz E.
Osborn, Earl D.
Osborn, Frederick H.
Osborn, William H.
Osborne, Stanley de J.
Ostrander, F. Taylor, Jr.

Overby, Andrew N.
Overton, Douglas W.

Pace, Frank, Jr.
Page, Howard W.
Page, John H.
Page, Robert G.
Pagnamenta, G.
Paley, William S.
Parker, Philo W.
Patterson, Ellmore C.
Patterson, Frederick D.
Patterson, Morehead
Patterson, Richard C., Jr.
Payne, Frederick B.
Payne, Samuel B.
Payson, Charles Shipman
Peardon, Thomas P.
Peffer, Nathaniel
Pennoyer, Paul G.
Peretz, Don
Perkins, James A.
Perkins, Roswell B.
Peters, C. Brooks
Petersen, Gustav H.
Petschek, Stephen R.
Phillips, Christopher H.
Pierce, William C.
Pierson, Warren Lee
Pifer, Alan
Pike, H. Harvey
Plimpton, Francis T. P.

Poletti, Charles
Polk, Judd
Poor, Henry V.
Potter, Robert S.
Powers, Joshua B.
Pratt, H. Irving, Jr.
Proudfit, Arthur T.

Quigg, Philip W.

Rabi, Isidor I.
Rathbone, M. J.
Ray, George W., Jr.
Reber, Samuel
Redmond, Roland L.
Reed, Philip D.
Reeves, Jay B. L.
Reid, Ogden
Reid, Whitelaw
Rheinstein, Alfred
Richardson, Arthur Berry
Richardson, Dorsey
Richardson, John R., Jr.
Riegelman, Harold
Ripley, Joseph P.
Roberts, George
Roberts, Henry L.
Robinson, Geroid T.
Robinson, Leland Rex
Rockefeller, David
Rockefeller, John D., 3rd
Rockhill, Victor E.

Rodriguez, Vincent A.
Rogers, Lindsay
Roosevelt, George Emlen
Root, Elihu, Jr.
Root, Oren
Roper, Elmo
Rosenberg, James N.
Rosenman, Samuel I.
Rosenstiel, Lewis
Rosenwald, William
Rosinski, Herbert
Ross, Emory
Ross, T. J.
Rouse, Robert G.
Royce, Alexander B.
Ruebhausen, Oscar M.
Rush, Kenneth
Rustow, Dankwart A.

Sachs, Alexander
Sachs, Howard J.
Saltzman, Charles E.
Samuels, Nathaniel
Sargeant, Howland H.
Sargent, Noel
Sarnoff, Brig. Gen. David
Sawin, Melvin E.
Schaffner, Joseph Halle
Schapiro, J. Salwyn
Scherman, Harry
Schiff, John M.
Schiller, A. Arthur

Schilthuis, Willem C.
Schmidt, Herman J.
Schmoker, J. Benjamin
Schwartz, Harry
Schwarz, Frederick A. O.
Scott, John
Sedwitz, Walter J.
Seligman, Eustace
Seymour, Whitney North
Sharp, George C.
Sharp, James H.
Shea, Andrew B.
Sheffield, Frederick
Shepard, David A.
Shepard, Frank P.
Shepardson, Whitney H.
Shepherd, Howard C.
Sherbert, Paul C.
Sherman, Irving H.
Shields, Murray
Shields, W. Clifford
Shirer, William L.
Shute, Benjamin R.
Siegbert, Henry
Sims, Albert G.
Slater, Joseph E.
Slawson, John
Sloan, Alfred P., Jr.
Smith, Carleton Sprague
Smith, David S.
Smith, Hayden N.
Smith, W. Mason, Jr.

Smull, J. Barstow
Solbert, Peter O. A.
Sonne, H. Christian
Soubry, E. E.
Spaght, Monroe E.
Spang, Kenneth M.
Spencer, Percy C.
Spofford, Charles M.
Stackpole, Stephen H.
Stebbins, James H.
Stebbins, Richard P.
Stern, H. Peter
Stevenson, Adlai E.
Stevenson, John R.
Stewart, Robert McLean
Stillman, Chauncey
Stillman, Ralph S.
Stinebower, Leroy D.
Stoddard, George D.
Stokes, Isaac N. P.
Stone, Shepard
Straka, Jerome A.
Straus, Donald B.
Straus, Jack I.
Straus, Oscar S.
Straus, Ralph I.
Straus, R. Peter
Strauss, Simon D.
Strong, Benjamin
Sulzberger, Arthur Hays
Swatland, Donald C.

Swingle, William S.
Swope, Gerard, Jr.

Tannenbaum, Frank
Tannenwald, Theodore
Thomas, H. Gregory
Thompson, Earle S.
Thompson, Kenneth W.
Tibby, John
Tinker, Edward Laroque
Tomlinson, Roy E.
Townsend, Edward
Townsend, Oliver
Traphagan, J. C.
Travis, Martin B., Jr.
Trippe, Juan Terry
Truman, David B.
Tweedy, Gordon B.

Uzielli, Giorgio

Van Dusen, Rev. Henry P.
von Mehren, Robert B.
Voorhees, Tracy S.

Walker, Joseph, Jr.
Walkowicz, T. F.
Wallace, Schuyler C.
Warburg, Eric M.
Warburg, Frederick M.
Warburg, James P.
Ward, Thomas E.

Warfield, Ethelbert
Warren, John Edwin
Wasson, Donald
Wasson, R. Gordon
Watson, Arthur K.
Watson, Thomas J., Jr.
Wauchope, Rear Adm. George
Weaver, Sylvester L., Jr.
Webster, Bethuel M.
Welch, Leo D.
Wellborn, Vice Adm. Charles, Jr.
Wernimont, Kenneth
Wheeler, Walter H., Jr.
Whidden, Howard P.
Whipple, Taggart
Whipple, Brig. Gen. William
White, Frank X.
White, H. Lee
White, Theodore H.
Whitman, H. H.
Whitney, John Hay
Whitridge, Arnold
Wight, Charles A.
Wilkinson, Col. Lawrence
Willcox, Westmore
Williams, Langbourne M.
Willits, Joseph H.
Wilson, John D.
Wilson, Orme
Wilson, Philip D.
Wingate, Henry S.
Winslow, Richard S.

Wood, Bryce
Woodward, Donald B.
Woodyatt, Philip
Woolley, Knight
Wright, Harry N.
Wriston, Henry M.
Wriston, Walter B.

Yost, Charles W.
Young, John M.

Zurcher, Arnold J.

Non-Resident Members

Acheson, Dean
Achilles, Theodore C.
Adams, Roger
Agar, Herbert
Akers, Anthony B.
Allen, Raymond B.
Allyn, S. C.
Amory, Robert, Jr.
Anderson, Dillon
Anderson, Vice Adm. George
Anderson, Roger E.
Anderson, Gen. Samuel E.
Armstrong, John A.
Atherton, J. Ballard
Attwood, William
Auld, George P.

Babcock, Maj. Gen. C. Stanton
Badeau, John S.
Baker, George P.
Ball, George W.
Ballou, George T.
Barghoorn, Frederick C.
Barker, James M.
Barnett, Robert W.
Barrows, Leland
Bartholomew, Dana T.
Bass, Robert P., Jr.
Bassow, Whitman
Bateman, William H.
Bates, Marston
Bator, Francis M.
Bayne, Edward Ashley
Bechtel, S. D.
Bell, Holley Mack
Benda, Harry J.
Bennett, Martin Toscan
Bergson, Abram
Berkner, L. V.
Bernstein, Edward M.
Betts, Brig. Gen. Thomas J.
Bissell, Richard M., Jr.
Black, Cyril E.
Black, Col. Edwin F.
Black, Eugene R.
Blackie, William B.
Bliss, C. I.
Bliss, Robert Woods
Bloomfield, Lincoln P.

Blum, Robert
Boeschenstein, Harold
Bohlen, Charles E.
Bonesteel, Maj. Gen. C. H. 3rd
Boothby, Albert C.
Borton, Hugh
Bowie, Robert R.
Bowles, Chester
Braden, Thomas W.
Bradfield, Richard
Braisted, Paul J.
Brett, George P., Jr.
Brewster, Kingman, Jr.
Briggs, Ellis O.
Brinton, Crane
Bristol, William M.
Bronwell, Arthur
Brophy, Gerald B.
Brorby, Melvin
Bross, John A.
Brown, Irving
Brown, Sevellon, 3rd
Brown, William O.
Bruce, David K. E.
Brundage, Percival F.
Bruton, Henry J.
Bundy, Harvey H.
Bundy, McGeorge
Bundy, William P.
Burgess, W. Randolph
Byrne, James MacGregor

Byrnes, Robert F.
Byroade, Henry A.

Cabot, John M.
Cabot, Louis W.
Cabot, Thomas D.
Caldwell, Robert G.
Calkins, Hugh
Camp, Jack L.
Campbell, Kenneth H.
Canfield, Franklin O.
Caraway, Lt. Gen. Paul W.
Carpenter, W. Samuel, 3rd
Carter, William D.
Cary, William L.
Case, Clifford P.
Case, Everett N.
Chapin, Selden
Chapman, John F.
Cheever, Daniel S.
Cherrington, Ben M.
Childs, Marquis
Cisler, Walker L.
Clark, Ralph L.
Clayton, W. L.
Cleveland, Harlan
Clough, Ernest T.
Coffey, Joseph Irving
Cohen, Benjamin V.
Cole, Charles W.
Collbohm, F. R.
Collyer, John L.

Conlon, Richard P.
Conrad, Brig. Gen. Bryan
Considine, Rev. John J., M. M.
Coons, Arthur G.
Copeland, Lammot du Pont
Corson, John J.
Costello, William A.
Cotting, Charles E.
Cowen, Myron M.
Cowles, John
Crane, Winthrop Murray, 3rd
Creighton, Albert M.
Cross, James E.
Crotty, Homer D.
Crowe, Philip K.
Culbertson, Col. William S.
Curran, Jean A., Jr.
Curtis, Edward P.

Dangerfield, Royden
Darlington, Charles F.
David, Donald K.
Davidson, Alfred E.
Davidson, Carter
Davies, Fred A.
Davis, Nathanael V.
Dean, Edgar P.
Decker, William C.
de Guigne, Christian, 3rd
da Kiewiet, C. W.
de Krafft, William
Deming, Frederick L.

Despres, Emile
Deuel, Wallace R.
Deutch, Michael J.
Dewhurst, J. Frederic
Dexter, Byron
Dickey, John S.
Dillon, C. Douglas
Dodds, Harold Willis
Dollard, Charles
Donkin, McKay
Donnell, James C., 2nd
Donnelly, Maj. Gen. Harold C.
Dorr, Russell H.
Douglas, Donald W., Jr.
Draper, William H., Jr.
Drummond, Roscoe
Ducas, Robert
Duce, James Terry
Duke, Angier Biddle
Dulles, Allen W.
Dunn, Frederick S.

Eckstein, Alexander
Edelstein, Julius C. C.
Edwards, A. R.
Edwards, William H.
Einaudi, Mario
Einstein, Lewis
Eisenhower, Dwight D.
Elliott, Byron K.
Elliott, Randle
Elliott, William Y.

Elsey, George M.
Elson, Robert T.
Emeny, Brooks
Emerson, E. A.
Emerson, Rupert
Eppert, Ray R.
Estabrook, Robert H.
Ethridge, Mark
Evans, J. K.
Everton, John Scott

Fainsod, Merle
Fairbank, John King
Fairbanks, Douglas
Farmer, Thomas L.
Fay, Sidney B.
Feely, Edward F.
Feis, Herbert
Ferguson, John H.
Finkelstein, Lawrence S.
Finlay, Luke W.
Finletter, Thomas K.
Firestone, Harvey S., Jr.
Fischer, George
Fisher, Edgar J.
Fleischmann, Julius
Fleming, Lamar, Jr.
Follis, R. G.
Ford, Guy Stanton
Ford, Thomas K.
Foster, Austin T.
Foster, William C.

Fowler, Henry H.
Foy, Fred C.
Frank, Isaiah
Frank, Joseph A.
Frankfurter, Felix
Fredericks, J. Wayne
Free, Lloyd A.
Fuller, Carlton P.
Furber, Holden
Furniss, Edgar S., Jr.

Galbraith, J. Kenneth
Gallagher, Charles F.
Gannett, Lewis S.
Gardiner, Arthur Z.
Gardner, Richard N.
Garner, Robert L.
Garthoff, Raymond L.
Gaud, William S.
Gavin, Lt. Gen. James M.
Gaylord, Bradley
Geier, Frederick V.
Geier, Paul E.
Gerhart, Lt. Gen. John K.
Giffin, Brig. Gen. Sidney F.
Gilbert, Carl J.
Gilbert, H. N.
Gilchrist, Huntington
Gillin, John P.
Gilpatric, Roswell L.
Gleason, S. Everett
Glennan, T. Keith

Goheen, Robert F.

Goldberg, Arthur J.

Goodhart, Arthur L.

Goodpaster, Maj. Gen. Andrew J.

Goodrich, Carter

Gordon, Lincoln

Gornick, Alan L.

Gorter, Wytze

Gould, Laurence M.

Graham, Philip L.

Grant, James P.

Grant, Maj. Gen. U. S., 3rd

Gray, Gordon

Green, Joseph C.

Greene, A. Crawford

Greene, James C.

Greenewalt, Crawford H.

Greenwood, Heman

Griffith, William E.

Griswold, A. Whitney

Grove, Curtiss C.

Gruenther, Gen. Alfred M.

Gullion, Edmund A.

Halle, Louis J., Jr.

Hamilton, Fowler

Hamilton, Maj. Gen. Pierpont M.

Hammonds, Oliver W.

Hansell, Gen. Haywood S., Jr.

Harbison, Frederick

Harriman, W. Averell

Harris, Irving B.

Harsch, Joseph. C.
Hart, Augustin S.
Hartley, Robert W.
Haskell, Broderick
Haskins, Caryl P.
Hauck, Arthur A.
Haviland, H. Field, Jr.
Hayes, Samuel P.
Hays, Brooks
Hays, John T.
Heffelfinger, Totton P., 2nd
Heilperin, Michael A.
Heintzen, Harry L.
Heinz, H. J., 2nd
Henderson, Loy W.
Henkin, Louis
Henry, David Dodds
Herter, Christian A.
Hill, George Watts
Hitch, Charles J.
Hofer, Philip
Hoffman, Michael L.
Hoffman, Paul G.
Holborn, Hajo
Holland, William L.
Holmes, Julius C.
Homer, Arthur B.
Hook, George V.
Hoover, Calvin B.
Hoover, Herbert
Hoover, Herbert, Jr.
Hopkins, D. Luke

Hopper, Bruce C.
Hornbeck, Stanley K.
Hoskins, Halford L.
Hoskins, Harold B.
Houghton, Amory
Hovde, Frederick L.
Hovey, Allan, Jr.
Howard, Graeme K.
Howe, Walter
Hoyt, Edwin C., Jr.
Hoyt, Palmer
Huglin, Brig. Gen. H. C.
Humphrey, Hubert H.
Hunsberger, Warren S.
Hunt, James Ramsay, Jr.
Hunter, Clarence E.

Issawi, Charles P.
Iverson, Kenneth R.

Jackson, Elmore
Jackson, William H.
Jaffe, Sam A.
Jansen, Marius B.
Javits, Jacob K.
Jenney, John K.
Jessup, Philip C.
Johnson, Herschel V.
Johnson, Lester B.
Johnson, Robert L.
Johnston, Henry R.
Johnstone, W. H.

Jones, Peter T.
Jordan, Col, Amos A.
Jorden, William J.

Kahin, George McT.
Kaiser, Philip M.
Kamarck, Andrew M.
Katz, Milton
Katzenbach, Edward L., Jr.
Kauffman, James Lee
Kaufmann, William W.
Kelso, A. Donald
Kempner, Frederick C.
Kennan, George F.
Kerr, Clark
Killian, James R., Jr.
Kimberly, John H.
King, James E., Jr.
King, John A., Jr.
Kinkaid, Adm. Thomas C.
Kintner, Col. William R.
Kissinger, Henry A.
Knight, Douglas
Knorr, Klaus
Kohler, Foy D.
Kohler, Walter J.
Korbel, Josef
Korol, Alexander G.
Kotschnig, Walter

Labouisse, Henry R.
Ladejinsky, Wolf

Lamson, Roy, Jr.
Landis, James M.
Langer, Paul F.
Langer, William L.
Langsam, Walter Consuelo
Lanham, Maj. Gen. Charles T.
Lansdale, Gen. Edward G.
Larson, Jens Frederick
Lasswell, Harold D.
Latourette, Kenneth S.
Lattimore, Owen
Lawrence, David
Lawrence, W. H.
Laybourne, Lawrence E.
Laylin, John G.
Leddy, John M.
Lee, Charles Henry
Leghorn, Richard S.
Lemnitzer, Gen. L. L.
Leslie, Donald S.
Lesueur, Larry
Levine, Irving R.
Levy, Marion J., Jr.
Lewis, Herbert
Lewis, Wilmarth S.
Lichtenstein, Walter
Lincoln, Col. G. A.
Linder, Harold F.
Lindley, Ernest K.
Lindsay, Franklin A.
Lindsay, John V.
Lindsay, Lt. Gen. Richard C.

Linebarger, Paul M. A.
Lingelbach, William E.
Lingle, Walter L., Jr.
Lippmann, Walter
Litchfield, Edward H.
Little, Herbert S.
Little, L. K.
Lockard, Derwood W.
Locke, Edwin A., Jr.
Lockwood, William W.
Lodge, George Cabot
Loomis, Robert H.
Lunt, Samuel D.
Lyon, E. Wilson

McCabe, Thomas B.
McClintock, Robert M.
McCone, John Alex
McCormack, Maj. Gen. J., Jr.
McCracken, Paul W.
McCutcheon, John D.
McDougal, Edward D., Jr.
McDougal, Myres S.
McFarland, Ross A.
McGee, Gale W.
McGhee, George C.
McKay, Vernon
McKittrick, Thomas H.
McLaughlin, Donald H.
McArthur, Douglas, 2nd
MacChesney, A. Brunson, 3rd
MacDonald, J. Carlisle

MacVeagh, Lincoln
Machold, William F.
Maddox, William P.
Maddux, Maj. Gen. H. R.
Mallinson, Harry
Mallory, George W.
Manning, Bayless
Marcus, Stanley
Marshall, Charles B.
Martin, Edwin M.
Martin, William McC., Jr.
Masland, John W.
Mason, Edward S.
Mathews, William R.
Maximov, Andre
May, Oliver
Mayer, Ferdinand L.
Mayer, Gerald M.
Meagher, Robert F.
Meck, John F.
Menke, John R.
Merchant, Livingston T.
Merillat, H. C. L.
Merriwether, Duncan
Metcalf, George R.
Meyer, Charles A.
Meyer, Clarence E.
Meyer, Cord, Jr.
Milbank, Robbins
Miller, Francis P.
Miller, William B.
Millikan, Clark B.

Millikan, Max F.
Millis, John S.
Minor, Harold B.
Mitchell, James P.
Moore, Hugh
Moran, William E., Jr.
Morgan, George A.
Morgan, Shepard
Morgenstern, Oskar
Morgenthau, Hans J.
Mott, John L.
Mudd, Henry T.
Munoz Marin, Luis
Munro, Dana G.
Munson, Henry Lee
Murphy, Donald R.
Murphy, Franklin D.
Murphy, Robert
Murrow, Edward R.
Myers, Denys P.

Nathan, Robert R.
Nelson, Fred M.
Neumann, Sigmund
Newman, Richard T.
Newton, Quigg, Jr.
Nichols, Calvin J.
Niebuhr, Reinhold
Nitze, Paul H.
Nixon, Richard M.
Nover, Barnet

Noyes, W. Albert, Jr.
Nuveen, John

Oakes, George W.
Oelman, R. S.
Oppenheimer, J. Robert
Orchard, John E.
Osborne, Lithgow
Owen, Garry

Paffrath, Leslie
Palmer, Norman D.
Pantzer, Kurt F.
Park, Richard L.
Parker, Barrett
Parsons, John C.
Patterson, Gardner
Paul, Norman S.
Pelzer, Karl J.
Penfield, James K.
Perera, Guido R.
Perkins, Courtland D.
Perkins, Milo
Petersen, Howard C.
Phillips, William
Phleger, Herman
Piquet, Howard S.
Poque, L. Welch
Polk, William R.
Pool, Ithiel deSola
Power, Thomas F., Jr.
Prance, P. F. A.

Preston, Jerome
Price, Don K.
Pritchard, Ross J.
Prizer, John B.
Prochnow, Herbert V.
Pulling, Edward S.
Pusey, Nathan M.
Pye, Lucien W.

Radway, Laurence I.
Ravenholt, Albert
Reinhardt, G. Frederick
Reischauer, Edwin O.
Reitzel, William
Rennie, Wesley F.
Reston, James B.
Rich, John H., Jr.
Richardson, David B.
Ridgway, Gen. Matthew B.
Riefler, Winfield W.
Ries, Hans A.
Riley, Edward C.
Ripley, S. Dillon, 2nd.
Rivkin, Arnold
Robinson, Donald H.
Rockefeller, Nelson A.
Rogers, James Grafton
Romualdi, Serafino
Roosa, Robert V.
Roosevelt, Kermit
Roosevelt, Nicholas
Rosengarten, Adolph G., Jr.

Ross, Michael
Rostow, Eugene V.
Rostow, Walt W.
Rusk, Dean
Russell, Donald S.
Ryan, John T., Jr.

Salomon, Irving
Satterthwaite, Joseph C.
Sawyer, John E.
Schaetzel, J. Robert
Schelling, T. C.
Schlesinger, Arthur M., Jr.
Schmidt, Adolph W.
Schneider, Hubert A.
Schorr, Daniel L.
Schuyler, Gen. C. V. R.
Schwab, William B.
Schwebel, Stephen M.
Scott, William Ryland
Seymour, Charles
Seymour, Forrest W.
Sharp, Walter R.
Sharpe, Henry D., Jr.
Shaw, G. Howland
Shearer, Warren W.
Sheean, Vincent
Shishkin, Boris
Shulman, Marshall D.
Shuster, George
Simons, Hans
Simpson, John L.

Slocum, John J.
Smith, Everett R.
Smith, Gerard G.
Smith, H. Alexander
Smith, Adm. Harold Page
Smith, Robert W.
Smithies, Arthur
Smyth, Henry DeW.
Snyder, Richard C.
Sontag, Raymond James
Soth, Lauren K.
Southard, Frank A., Jr.
Spaatz, Gen. Carl
Speers, Rev. Theodore C.
Spencer, John H.
Spiegel, Harold R.
Sprague, Mansfield D.
Sprague, Robert C.
Sproul, Robert G.
Sprout, Harold
Staley, Eugene
Stanton, Edwin F.
Stason, E. Blythe
Stasson, Harold E.
Stein, Eric
Stein, Harold
Stephens, Claude O.
Sterling, J. E. Wallace
Stevenson, William E.
Stewart, Col. George
Stewart, Robert Burgess
Stilwell, Col. Richard G.

Stone, Donald C.
Stowe, Leland
Straton, Julius A.
Straus, Robert Kenneth
Strauss, Lewis L.
Strausz-Hupe, Robert
Strayer, Joseph R.
Struble, Adm. A. D.
Sulzberger, C. L.
Sunderland, Thomas E.
Surrey, Walter Sterling
Sweetser, Arthur
Swensrud, Sidney A.
Swihart, James W.
Symington, W. Stuart

Talbot, Phillips
Tanham, George K.
Tapp, Jesse W.
Taylor, George E.
Taylor, Gen. Maxwell D.
Taylor, Wayne Chatfield
Teller, Edward
Templeton, Richard H.
Tennyson, Leonard B.
Thayer, Charles W.
Thayer, Robert H.
Thornburg, Max W.
Thorp, Willard L.
Trager, Frank N.
Triffin, Robert
Trowbridge, Alexander B.

Truscott, Gen. Lucian K., Jr.
Tuck, William Hallam

Ulmer, Alfred C., Jr.
Upgren, Arthur R.

Valentine, Alan
Van Cleve, Thomas C.
Van Slyck, DeForest
Van Stirum, John
Vernon, Raymond
Viner, Jacob

Wadsworth, James J.
Wait, Richard
Wallich, Henry C.
Walmsley, Walter N.
Wanger, Walter
Ward, Rear Adm. Chester
Warren, Shields
Washburn, Abbott
Watkins, Ralph J.
Weeks, Edward
Wells, Herman B.
Westmoreland, Maj. Gen. W. C.
Westphal, Albert C. F.
Wheeler, Oliver P.
Whitaker, Arthur P.
White, Gilbert F.
White, John Campbell
Whiteford, William K.
Wiesner, Jerome B.

Wilbur, Brayton
Wilbur, C. Martin
Wilcox, Francis O.
Wilcox, Robert B.
Wild, Payson S., Jr.
Wilde, Frazar B.
Wilds, Walter W.
Williams, John H.
Wilmerding, Lucius, Jr.
Wilson, Carroll L.
Wilson, Howard E.
Wilson, O. Meredith
Wimpfheimer, Jacques
Winton, David J.
Wisner, Frank G.
Wohl, Elmer P.
Wohlstetter, Albert
Wolfers, Arnold
Wood, Harleston R.
Wriggins, W. Howard
Wright, Adm. Jerauld
Wright, Quincy
Wright, Theodore P.
Wyzanski, Charles E., Jr.

Yntema, Theodore O.
Young, Kenneth T.
Young, T. Cuyler

Zellerbach, J. D.

APPENDIX II.

ATLANTIC UNION COMMITTEE MEMBERSHIP ROSTER
This membership list was published by the Atlantic Union Committee in December, 1960. "CFR" in parentheses after a name is an editorial indication that the person is also a member of the Council on Foreign Relations. No other biographical information is given for CFR members. The biographical information, on the AUC members who are not also CFR members, was taken from Who's Who and/or the American Dictionary of Biography.

Abbott, Mrs. George

Abend, Hallet

Achilles, Paul S., Chairman of the Board, Psychological Corporation; Board member, Eastman-Kodak Company

Adams, James D., Partner, McCutchen, Doyle, Brown & Enersen, Lawyers, San Francisco

Adams, Hon. Paul L., Attorney General, State of Michigan

Agar, Herbert (CFR)

Agnew, Albert C.

Aiken, Hon. Paul C., former Assistant Postmaster General of the U. S.

Alexander, Mrs. Sadie T. M.

Allen, H. Julian, General Manager, Paris Office, Morgan Guaranty Trust Company

Allen, Dr. Max P.

Alvord, Ellsworth C., Member, law firm of Alvord & Alvord, Washington, D. C.; Board member, General Dynamics Corp., Smith-Corona, Inc.

Amen, John Harlan, Associate Trial Counsel, Nurnburg War Criminals Trials; Member, Amen, Weisman & Butler, New York City

Amory, Copley

Anderson, Don

Anderson, Eugene N., Professor of History, University of Southern California at Los Angeles

Anderson, Mrs. Eugene

Anderson, Eugenie Former Ambassador to Denmark

Anderson, Maj. Gen. Frederick L. Trustee, Rand Corp.

Anderson Dr. Paul R., President, Chatham College, Pittsburgh

Anderson Steve

Anderson, Victor E., Former Governor of Nebraska

Andrews, Mark Edwin, President, Second M. E. Andrews, Ltd., Houston

Andrews, Dr. Stanley, Executive Director, Kellogg Foundation

Apperson John W.

Armour, Norman (CFR)

Armstrong, George S., President, George S. Armstrong & Co., New York City, Trustee, Committee for Economic Development

Armstrong, O. K., Member, Editorial Staff Reader's Digest, Former Congressman; Founder, Department of Journalism, University of Florida

Arnold, Remmie L.

Arnold, Thurman, Former U. S. Assistant Attorney General

Arzt, Dr. Max, President, Jewish Theological Seminary

Atherton, Warren H., Past National Commander, American Legion

Aurner, Dr. Robert R., President, Aurner & Associates, Carmel, California

Babian, Haig

Bache, Harold L., Sr., Senior Partner, Bache & Co., New York City

Bacon, Mrs. Robert Low, Chairman, Administration Liaison Committee, National Federation of Republican Women

Bagwell, Dr. Paul D., Past President, U. S. Junior Chamber of Commerce

Baker, Dr. Benjamin M., Jr.

Baker, Mrs. Frank C.

Baker, Rev. Richard, Bishop, Episcopal Diocese of North Carolina; Member, General Board, National Council of Churches

Balduf, Dr. Emery W.

Baldwin, Henry P., Vice President, Water Power & Paper Co., Wisconsin; Member, National Board, National Conference of Christians and Jews, Chairman, Brotherhood Week, 1956

Baldwin, Howard C., Chairman of the Board of Standard Federal Savings & Loan Association, Detroit; Vice President and Trustee, The Kresge Foundation, Member, Board of Publications, Methodist Church

Baldwin, Hon. Raymond E., Former U. S. Senator and Governor of Connecticut

Ball, George (CFR)

Ball, Hon, Joseph H., Former U. S. Senator from Minnesota

Banning, Mrs. Margaret

Barclay, Dr. Thomas Swain, Professor of Political Science, Stanford University, Member, National Municipal League; Member, American Delegation to Negotiate the Peace, 1919

Barinowski, R. E.

Barnes, Julius H. (CFR)

Barrows, Mrs. Ira

Bartlett, Lynn M., Superintendent of Public Schools, State of Michigan; Former President, National Education Assn.

Barzun, Jacques, Dean of Faculty and Provost, Columbia. University; Author, Historian, Musicologist

Batcheller, Hiland G., Chairman of the Board, Allegheny-Ludlum Steel Corp.

Bates, Dr. Rosalind Goodrich, Past President, International Federation of Women Lawyers

Battle, Laurie C., Former Congresswoman from Alabama

Baukhage, H. R., Consulting Editor, Army Times Publishing Company; Radio Commentator

Bayne, The Rt. Rev. Stephen F., Jr., Executive Officer, Anglican Communion

Beaton, Harold D.

Becker, Herman D.

Becker, Ralph E., Past Chairman, Young Republican National Federation

Beckett, Mrs. R. Capel

Beeley, Dr. Arthur L. Dean Emeritus, School of Social Work, University of Utah; Official, National Association for Mental Health

Belknap, William

Bell, Edgar D.

Bell, Robert C., Jr.

Belsheim, Dr. Edmund O., Dean, College of Law, University of Nebraska

Benedict, Harry E. (CFR)

Bennet, Augustus W.

Bennett, Admiral Andrew C.

Benson, Dr. Oscar A., President, Augustana Lutheran Church

Bertholf, Dr. Lloyd M., President, Illinois Wesleyan University

Biddle, George

Bidgood, Dr. Lee

Bingham, Alfred M.

Birkhead, Kenneth M.

Bishop, Robert J.

Bissantz, Edgar

Bixler, J. Seelye, President, Colby College, Maine; Former Dean, Harvard Divinity School

Blackwelder, Dr. Eliot, Professor Emeritus of Geology, Stanford University

Blair, Paxton, Solicitor General, State of New York

Blanchard, Rt. Rev. Roger W.

Blanshard, Dr. Brand, Professor of Philosophy, Yale University

Blewett, Edward Y., President, Westbrook Junior College, Maine; Former Dean of Liberal Arts, University of New Hampshire

Bliss, Robert Woods (CFR)

Boas, Dr. George, Professor of Philosophy, John Hopkins University

Boekel, William A.

Boggs, Dr. Marion A., Moderator, Presbyterian Church, U.S.

Bohn, William E.

Bonds, Dr. Alfred B., Jr., President, Baldwin-Wallace College, Ohio

Borsody, Dr. Stephen

Bowles, Mrs. Istvan

Bowles, Chester (CFR)

Boyd, Brig. Gen. Ralph G.

Bradley, Rev. Preston, Founder and Pastor, People's Unitarian Church, Chicago

Braendel, Helmuth G.

Brand, Hon. James T., Associate Justice, Oregon Supreme Court

Brandt, Dr. Karl, Director, Food Research Institute, Stanford University

Brannan, Charles F., Former U. S. Secretary of Agriculture

Branscomb, Dr. Harvie, Chancellor, Vanderbilt University

Braucher, Robert, Professor of Law, Harvard University

Breckinridge, John B.

Brees, Orlo M.

Briefs, Dr. Goetz A., Professor of Labor Economics, Georgetown University

Briscoe, John D.

Bronk, Dr. Detlev W. (CFR)

Brooklings, Mrs. Robert S., Philanthropist

Brown, John Nicholas, Former Under Secretary of Navy for Air

Brown, Julius A.

Brown, Mary Agnes, Member, U. S. Board of Veterans Appeals

Brown, Prentiss M., Former U. S. Senator from Michigan

Brown, Thomas Cook, Editor Emeritus, Buffalo Courier-Express; Member, Foreign Policy Association; Member Advisory Board, Buffalo Council on World Affairs

Browning, Gordon

Brundage, Hon. Percival F. (CFR)

Bryson, Dr. Lyman (CFR)

Bullis, Harry A. (CFR)

Bunker, Arthur H. (CFR)

Bunker, Hon. Ellsworth (CFR)

Bunting, Dr. J. Whitney, Professor of Finance, New York University; Research Consultant, General Electric Company; Former President, Oglethorpe University

Burch, Lucius E., Jr.

Burling, Edward B., Partner, Covington & Burling, Lawyers, Washington, D. C.

Burnett, Leo, Chairman of the Board, Leo Burnett Company; Director, Advertising Council, Chicago Better Business Bureau; Trustee, American Heritage Foundation

Burns, Dr. Arthur F. (CFR)

Burns, James MacGregor, Professor of Political Science, Williams College

Burt, Katharine Newlin

Burwell, W. Russell, Vice Chairman Of the Board, Clevite Corp.; Past President, Cleveland Council on World Affairs

Cabot, Henry B. (CFR)

Cahn, Mrs. Moise S.

Caldwell, Dr. Frank H., President, Louisville Presbyterian Seminary

Caldwell, Dr. Harmon W., Chancellor, University System of Georgia

Caldwell, Dr. John T., Chancellor, North Carolina State College

Canaday, Ward M., President and Chairman of the Board, The Overland Corp.

Canfield, Cass (CFR)

Cantril, Dr. Hadley, Chairman, Institute for International Social Research, Princeton

Capra, Frank, Motion Picture Producer

Carlton, Doyle E., Former Governor of Florida

Carmichael, Dr. Oliver C. (CFR)

Carrington, Paul, Partner, Carrington, Johnson & Stephens, Lawyers, Dallas; Past President, Dallas Council on World Affairs; National Councilor, Boy Scouts of America; Trustee Southwest Legal Foundation, S.M.U.

Carter, Edward W., President, Broadway-Hale Stores, Inc., Los Angeles; Trustee, Committee for Economic Development; Member, Board of Regents, University of California

Carter, Hodding, Pulitzer Prize Editor, Greenville, Mississippi

Carter, John L.

Cary, Sheldon

Casey, Dr. Ralph D., Director Emeritus, School of Journalism, University of Minnesota

Catton, Bruce, Editor, American Heritage Magazine; Pulitzer Prize for History, 1954

Chabrak, Thomas

Chadwick, Stephen F., Past National Commander, American Legion

256

Chandler, Walter C., Former Congressman from Tennessee; Former Mayor of Memphis

Chenery, William L.

Chipps, Roy B.

Cisler, Walker L. (CFR)

Clagett, J. R.

Claypool, Mrs. J. Gordon

Clayton, William L. (CFR)

Clingman, Rt. Rev. Charles

Clothier, Dr. Robert C.

Clough, Dr. Shepard B., Director, Casa Italiana, Columbia University

Code, Dr. Charles F., Professor of Physiology, University of Minnesota; Consultant, Mayo Clinic

Coe, Dr. Albert Buckner, Official, National Council of Churches; Delegate to 1st and 2nd World Council of Churches

Coffee, John M.

Cohen, Harry, Retired Surgeon; Former Editor, American Jewish Cyclopedia; Editor-in-Chief, American Jews: Their Lives and Achievements

Cole, Wilton D., Chairman of the Board, Crowell-Collier Publishing Company

Collier, W. Edwin

Compton, Dr. Arthur H., Professor, Washington University, St. Louis; Nobel Prize in Physics, 1927; Former Co-Chairman, National Conference of Christians and Jews; Former member, Committee for Economic Development; Former General Chairman, World Brotherhood; Dean Emeritus, Washington University, St. Louis

Compton, Dr. Wilson, Former President, State College of Washington; Chairman of the Board, Cameron Machine Co.; Director, International Council of Christian Leadership

Comstock, Alzada

Comstock, Louis K.

Cook, Lyle E.

Coons, Dr. Arthur Gardiner (CFR)

Corn, James F.

Corsi, Edward, Former Commissioner of Immigration and Naturalization

Cortney, Philip, Chairman, U. S. Council, International Chamber of Commerce; President, Coty, Inc. and Coty International

Cotton, Aylett B.

Cowles, Gardner (CFR)

Cox, C. R. (CFR)

Crane, Dr. Henry Hitt, Official, World Council of Churches

Crawford, Arthur L., Director, College of Mines & Minerals, University of Utah

Cross, Dr. George L., President, University of Oklahoma

Crosswaith, Frank, Chairman, Negro Labor Committee

Crouch, Harry E.

Cruikshank, Nelson H., Director, Department of Social Security, AFL-CIO, Member, Federal Advisory Council, Department of Labor, Member, National Planning Association; Official, National Council of Churches

Cruse, Mrs. W. C.

Cutting, Fulton (CFR)

Dail, Charles C.

Daltry, Joseph S., Director, Graduate Summer School for Teachers, Wesleyan University, Connecticut

Dandridge, Rt. Rev. E. P.

Darden, Hon. Colgate W., Retired President, University of Virginia; Former Governor of Virginia; Former Congressman from Virginia

Darling, Jay N., Retired Cartoonist, New York Herald-Tribune; Pulitzer Prize, 1923, 1942

Daugherty, Paul E.

Davidson, Dr. Philip G., President, University of Louisville

Davies, Mrs. A. Powell

Davis, Chester C., Associate Director, Ford Foundation

Davis, J. Lionberger

Davis, Dr. Stanton Ling

Davis, William H. (CFR)

Dawson, John P., Professor of Law, Harvard University; Former Professor of Law, University of Michigan

Day, Dean John W.

Deane, Maj. Gen. John R., Former Chief, American Military Mission to U.S.S.R.

Debevoise, Thomas M. (CFR)

Deinard, Amos S.

deKiewiet, Dr. C. W. (CFR)

Dempsey, James

Dennis, Don

De Pasquale, Judge Luigi

de Spoelberch, Mrs. Eric

D'Estournelles, Mrs. Julie

Devers, Gen. Jacob L., Retired Commander of Sixth Army Group

Dewhurst, Dr. J. Frederic (CFR)

Dickason, H. L.

Dickey, Dr. Frank G., President, University of Kentucky

Diemer, Dr. George W.

Dietz, Howard, Vice President, MGM

Dimock, Edward Jordan, Federal District Judge, Southern District of New York

Dodge, Cleveland E. (CFR)

Doman, Nicholas

Donohue, F. Joseph

Donovan, Dr. Herman L., President Emeritus, University of Kentucky

Donovan, James G., Former Congressman from New York; Director of the Federal Housing Administration, 1957-58

Dorothy, Mrs. Dorothy

Dorr, Dr. Harold M., Dean, State-wide Education, University of Michigan

Dorr, John V. N. (CFR)

Douglass, Dr. Paul F., Former President, American University

Draper, Maj. Gen. William H., Jr. (CFR)

Draughon, Dr. Ralph B., President, Alabama Polytechnic Institute (Auburn)

Dun, The Rt. Rev. Angus, Episcopal Bishop of Washington, D. C.; Former official of Federal Council of Churches

Dunbar, Charles E., Jr., Professor Emeritus of Law, Tulane University; Vice President, National Civil Service League

Duncan, Robert F.

Earnest, Dr. G. Brooks, President, Fenn College, Cleveland; Trustee, Cleveland Council on World Affairs

Eastvold, Dr. Seth C., First Vice President, Evangelical Lutheran Church

Eberstadt, Ferdinand (CFR)

Eccles, Marriner S., Former Chairman, Board of Governors, Federal Reserve System; Chairman of the Board, First Securities Corp.

Edge, Nelson J., Jr.

Edgren, Mrs. M. C.

Edmonds, Douglas L., Former Justice, Supreme Court of California

Edmunds, J. Ollie, President, John B. Stetson University, DeLand, Florida

Edson, Col. C. A.

Edwards, Horace H., City Manager, Richmond, Virginia; Campaign Manager, Roosevelt, 1936; General Director, National Democratic Campaigns 1940, 1944

Edwards, James E., President, Prairie Farmer Publishing Co., Radio Station WLS, Chicago

Eichleay, John W.

Elligett, Mrs. Raymond T.

Elliott, Dr. William M., Jr., Pastor, Highland Presbyterian Church, Dallas; former Chairman & Moderator, World Missions, Presbyterian Church, U. S.

Ellis, Dr. Calvert N., President, Juanita College, Pennsylvania

Ellis, Clyde T.

Ellis, Dr. Elmer, President, University of Missouri

Elmendorf, Armin

Emerson, E. A. (CFR)

Emrich, The Rt. Rev. Richard S. M., Episcopal Bishop of Michigan

Engel, Irving M., President, American Jewish Committee; Member, Law Firm of Engel, Judge, Miller, Sterling & Reddy, New York City

Erlanger, Milton S.

Estwing, Ernest

Ethridge, Mrs. Mark (husband in CFR)

Evjue, William T., Editor, Madison, Wisconsin, Capital-Times

Fairbanks, Douglas, Jr. (CFR)

Farley, Eugene Shedden, President, Wilkes College, Pennsylvania

Farnsley, Charles P., Lawyer, Former Mayor of Louisville, Kentucky

Feller, Karl F., President, International Union of United Brewery, Flour, Cereal, Soft Drink & Distillery Workers of America; Member, American Heritage Foundation

Ferguson, Charles W., Senior Editor, The Reader's Digest

Ferguson, Mrs. Walter

Fischer, Louis, Author, Foreign Correspondent; Authority on the Soviet Union, Spain and Mahatma Gandhi

Fisher, Kenneth

Fitch, H. M., Vice-president, American Air Filter Company

Fitz-Hugh, Col. Alexander

Flower, Henry C., Jr., Vice Chairman, J. Walter Thompson Co.

Flynt, Dr. Ralph C. M., Assistant U. S. Commissioner of Education; Former President, Atlantic Treaty Association

Folsom, Marion B. (CFR)

Forgan, J. Russell, Partner, Glore, Forgan & Co., Investments, Chicago; Board member, National Distillers Products Corp., Studebaker-Packard Corp., Borg-Warner Corp.

Foster, Dr. Luther H., President, Tuskegee Institute

Fowler, Earle B.

Francis, Clarence, Former Chairman of Board, General Foods Corp.

Freeman, Orville L., Secretary of Agriculture; Former Governor of Minnesota

Friedrich, Carl J., Eaton Professor of Government, Harvard University; Author

Fritchey, Clayton, Publisher, Northern Virginia Sun, Arlington; Director, Foreign Policy Association; Deputy Chairman, National Democratic Committee, 1952-61

Fuller, Alfred C., Chairman of Board, Fuller Brush Company

Fuller, Carlton P. (CFR)

Fuller, Dr. Richard E., President, Seattle Art Museum; Research Professor, University of Washington; Former Chairman, Northwest Division, Institute of Pacific Relations

Funk, Wilfred, Chairman, Wilfred Funk, Inc., Publishers; President, Funk & Wagnalls Company, Publishers

Furlong, Mrs. Margaret K.

Gammage, Dr. Grady, President, Arizona State University; Director, National Conference of Christians and Jews

Gannon, Rev. Robert I., S. J., Former President, Fordham University

Gape, Charles

Garwood, W. St. John, Former Justice, Supreme Court of Texas

Garwood, Mrs. W. St. John

Gaston, C. Marion

Gates, Hon. Artemus L. (CFR)

Gavin, Lt. Gen. James M. (CFR)

Gerstenfeld, Rabbi Norman, Washington (D.C.) Hebrew Congregation

Gettell, Dr. Richard Glenn, President, Mt. Holyoke College

Geyer, Bertram B., Retired Chairman of the Board, Geyer Advertising, Inc.

Gideonse, Dr. Harry D. (CFR)

Gifford, Miss Chloe, Past President, General Federation of Women's Clubs

Giles, Dr. Philip Randall, General Superintendent, Universalist Church of America

Gillette, Guy M., Former Senator from Iowa

Gilliam, Miss Elsie

Glenn, Dr. C. Leslie, Professor, Mental Health Institute, University of Michigan; Former Rector, St. John's Cathedral, Washington, D. C.; Former Rector, Christ Church, Cambridge, Massachusetts

Golden, Clinton S., Former Vice-President, United Steelworkers of America

Gorin, Louis J., Jr.

Gould, Dr. Laurence M. (CFR)

Grace, Miss Charity

Granger, Lester, Executive Secretary, National Urban League

Grew, Joseph C. (CFR)

Griffith, Dr. Ernest S., Dean, School of International Service, American University; Member, National Municipal League, American Association of Public Administrators; Former Chairman, National Conference of Christians and Jews; Former member, Board of Missions and Church Extension, Methodist Church; Director, Library of Congress Legislative Reference Service, 1940-1958

Gross, Dr. Mason W., President & Former Provost, Rutgers University

Grosse, Dr. Aristid V., President, Research Institute, Temple University

Grover, Allen (CFR)

Gulick, Dr. Robert L., Jr.

Hackett, Mrs. John R.

Haflich, Victor

Hager, Lawrence W., President, Owensboro, Kentucky Inquirer, Messenger, and Broadcasting Company

Hager, Dr. Walter E.

Hale, Robert, Former Member of Congress from Maine

Haley, Andrew G., Member Federal Communications Commission; Member, Society for Comparative Legislation & International Law

Hall, Dr. Clarence W., Editor, Reader's Digest

Hall, Hon. Fred, Former Governor of Kansas

Hallauer, Carl S., Chairman of the Board, Bausch & Lomb Optical Company

Halverson, Rev. Dr. W. Q.

Hamilton, G. E.

Hamlin, Chauncey J. (CFR)

Hammond, H. O.

Hancher, Dr. Virgil M., President, State University of Iowa

Hand, Dr. George H., Vice President, Southern Illinois University

Haralson, William

Harden, Dr. Edgar L., President, Northern Michigan College; Official, National Education Association

Hardin, Dr. Clifford M., Chancellor, University of Nebraska

Hardy, Grace C., M. D.

Hardy, Mrs. T. W., Sr.

Hare, James M.

Hargrave, Thomas J., Chairman, Eastman Kodak Company; Director, Executive Committee, Westinghouse Electric Corp.

Harless, Richard F.

Harmer, Miss Vera

Harmon, Dr. Henry Gadd, President, Drake University

Harriman, E. Roland (CFR)

Harriman, Lewis G., Chairman of the Board, Manufacturers & Traders Trust Company; President, M&T Discount Corp,; Founder, National Better Business Bureau; Member, Buffalo Council on World Affairs; Vice Chairman, University of Buffalo; Recipient, Brotherhood Citation, National Conference of Christians and Jews, 1956

Harris, Duncan G., Chairman of the Board, Brown, Harris, Stevens, Inc.; Director, Paramount Pictures Corp.

Harris, Morgan

Harris, Dr. Rufus Carrollton, President, Tulane University; Former Chairman of Board, Federal Reserve Bank, Atlanta; Trustee, Eisenhower Exchange Fellowships, Inc.

Harrison, W. B.

Hartley, Livingston

Hartung, Albert F., International President, International Woodworkers of America

Harvill, Dr. Richard A., President, University of Arizona

Hawley, James H., Jr.

Hayes, A. J., President, International Association of Machinists

265

Hayt, Miss Jessie

Hazard, Leland, Former Professor of Law, Carnegie Institute of Technology; Vice-President, Pittsburgh Plate Glass Co.

Healy, G. W. Jr., Past President, American Society of Newspaper Editors; Editor, New Orleans Times-Picayune; Director, The Advertising Council, Inc.

Heard, Gerald, Former Editor, The Realist, London; Former Lecturer, Oxford University; Founder, Irish Agriculture Co-operative Movement; Founder, English Co-operative Movement; Lecturer, New School of Social Research, New York City; Lecturer, Oberlin College

Heinsohn, Mrs. Robert A.

Heistand, Rt. Rev. John T.

Hellyer, Dr. David T.

Helmer, Borden

Helsley, Dr. Charles W.

Henderson, Ernest, President, Sheraton Corporation of America; Director, Boston World Affairs Council: Recipient, Brotherhood Citation, National Conference of Christians and Jews, 1959

Henry, Gerald B., Treasurer, Atlantic Union Committee

Henry, Rev. Leland B.

Herbert, R. Beverly

Herndon, Rev. Henry

Hertz, Rabbi Richard C.

Hesburgh, Rev. Theodore, C. S. C., President, University of Notre Dame; President, Institute of International Education; Member, Rockefeller Brothers Fund special studies project; Member, Civil Rights Commission of the United States

Hicks, Dr. Weimer K., President, Kalamazoo College

Hill, George Watts (CFR)

Hill, Herbert W., Professor of History, Dartmouth College; Director, New Hampshire Council on World Affairs

Hillis, Fred L.

Hilton, Conrad N., President, Hilton Hotels Corporation; Recipient, Brotherhood Citation, National Conference of Christians and Jews

Hilton, Dr. James H., President, Iowa State College of A & M Arts

Hines, Rt. Rev. John E., Episcopal Bishop of Texas

Hinshaw, David

Hobby, Mrs. Oveta Culp, Former U. S. Secretary of Health, Education & Welfare; President, Editor, Publisher, Houston Post; Trustee, American Assembly of Columbia University, Eisenhower Exchange Fellowships, Inc.; Director, Committee for Economic Development; Chairman of the Board, National Bank of Texas; Director, Mutual Insurance Company of New York

Hobson, Rt. Rev. Henry W., Episcopal Bishop of Southern Ohio

Hodes, Gen. Henry I., USA, Retired, Former Commander-in-Chief, U. S. Army, Europe

Hook, Sidney, Professor of Philosophy, New York University; Member, International Committee for Academic Freedom, John Dewey Society; Author: Heresy, Yes-Conspiracy, No, Common Sense and the Fifth Amendment, Marx and the Marxists

Hopkins, Dr. Ernest M. (CFR)

Horn, Dr. Francis H., President, University of Rhode Island; Former Director, Mental Hygiene Society of Maryland

Hornblow, Arthur, Jr., Motion Picture Producer, MGM

Horwood, Mrs. Henry A.

Hotchkis, Preston, Vice Chairman of the Board, Founders' Insurance Company; Member, Business Advisory Council

Houghton, Dr. Henry S.

Houston, Howard E.

Hovde, Dr. Frederick L. (CFR)

Howard, Ernest

Hoyt, Alfred O.

Hoyt, Palmer (CFR)

Hudson, C. B.

Hudson, Edward F., Advertising Consultant, Ted Bates & Co., New York City

Hudson, Paul H., Retired Executive Vice President, Empire Trust Company; Trustee, New York University

Humbert, Dr. Russell J., President, DePauw University, Indiana; Former official, Federal Council of Churches

Humphrey, Wolcott J.

Hunt, Dr. Charles W.

Hunt, Mrs. Walter S.

Hunter, Dr. Frederick

Hurd, Volney, Chief, Paris Bureau, Christian Science Monitor

Hutchinson, Martin B.

Isaacs, Norman E., Managing Editor, Louisville Times, Recipient, Journalism Medal, Southern Methodist University, 1955

Jacobson, Albert H., Insurance Broker; Past President, B'nai B'rith

Jacobson, Rabbi David

Jameson, Miss Betty

Jaszi, Dr. Oscar

Jenks, Almet, Author, The Huntsman at the Gate; The Second Chance

Jessel, George, Actor, Producer, Twentieth Century-Fox Films Corporation

Jessen, Herman F., Mink Farmer; National Democratic Committeeman from Wisconsin; Member, Foreign Policy Association, Americans for Democratic Action

Johnson, Dr. Eldon L., President, University of New Hampshire; Member, American Society of Public Administrators

Johnson, Herbert F., Chairman of the Board, S. C. Johnson & Son, Inc.; Trustee, Profit Sharing Research Foundation, Cornell University

Johnson, Iris Beatty

Johnson, Leroy, Former Congressman from California

Johnson, Dr. Robert L. (CFR)

Johnston, T. R.

Jones, Rt. Rev. Everett H., Episcopal Bishop of West Texas

Jordan, Dr. Wilbur K., President, Radcliffe College

Joseph, Franz Martin

Kallick, Sidney S., Chairman, National Board of Directors, Young Democratic Clubs of America

Kanzler, Ernest, Retired Chairman of the Board, Universal C. I. T. Credit Corporation; Member, Business Advisory Council, Committee for Economic Development

Kaplan, Dr. Joseph, Chairman, U. S. National Committee for International Geophysical Year; Professor of Physics, University of California; Member, Administrative Board, Hebrew Union College

Karelsen, Frank E., (Jr.) Partner, Karelsen & Karelsen, Lawyers, New York City; Commissioner, Community Mental Health Board, New York City; Member, Americans for Democratic Action; Honorary Chairman, American Jewish Committee

Katz, Donald L., Chairman of the Department of Chemical Engineering, University of Michigan

Keenan, Joseph H., Chairman, Department of Mechanical Engineering, Massachusetts Institute of Technology

Keith, William Scott

Keller, Oliver J., President & Manager, Radio Station WTAX, Springfield, Illinois

Kelley, Nicholas (CFR)

Kelly, Dr. Melvin J. (CFR)

Kennedy, Bishop Gerald, President, Methodist Council of Bishops; Member, Executive Committee, National Council of Churches

Keppel, A. R., President Catawba College, Salisbury, N. C.

Kerr, Dr. Clark, President, University of California

269

Ketchum, Carlton G., President, Ketchum, Inc, Campaign Director; Member, National Republican Finance Committee; Director, Association for Improvement of the Poor

Keyserling, Leon H., Former Chairman, President Truman's Council of Economic Advisers; President, Conference on Economic Progress

Kidder, George V., Dean of Liberal Arts, University of Vermont

King, Glen A.

Kinsolving, Rt. Rev. A. B., II, Episcopal Bishop of Arizona; Former President, Arizona Council of Churches

Kinsolving, Rev. Arthur Lee, Rector, St. James Episcopal Church, New York City; Dean, Convocation of Manhattan; Member, Department of Evangelism, National Council of Churches

Kirk, Adm. Alan Goodrich (CFR)

Kissinger, Dr. Henry A. (CFR)

Kizer, Benjamin H., Partner, Graves, Kizer & Gaiser, Lawyers, Spokane; Chairman, World Affairs Council of Inland Empire; Trustee, Institute of Pacific Relations; Former President, American Society of Planning Officials

Klutznick, Philip M., Vice Chairman, Illinois State Housing Board; Chairman of the International Council, B'nai B'rith; Member, National Council, Boy Scouts of America; Member, Commission on Money and Credit; Director, American Council to Improve Our Neighborhoods

Knight, O. A., President, Oil, Chemical & Atomic Workers International Union

Knutson, Coya, Former Congresswoman from Minnesota

Koessler, Horace H.

Kohn, Dr. Hans (CFR)

Kolthoff, Isaac M., Chairman, Department of Chemistry, University of Minnesota

Kreps, Dr. Theodore J., Professor of Business Economy, Stanford University

Kress, Ralph H.

Kretzmann, Dr. Otto P., President, Valparaiso University, Indiana

Kruger, Morris

Lamb, F. Gilbert

Lamont, Austin

Lancoine, Nelson, Past President, Young Democratic Clubs of America

Land, Adm. Emory S., President, Air Transport Association of America

Lang, Reginald D. (CFR)

Langlie, Arthur B., Former Governor of Washington

LaRue, D. W.

Lawrence, David L., Governor of Pennsylvania

Lederberg, Dr. Joshua, Nobel Prize Winner, Medicine & Physiology, 1958; Professor of Genetics, Stanford University

Lee, Dr. Russell V.

Lehman, Hon. Herbert H. (CFR)

Leibowitz, Judge Samuel S., Judge, Kings County Court, Brooklyn

Lemann, Mrs. Lucy Benjamin

Lerner, Abba P.

Levitas, Samuel M.

Lewis, Mrs. Dorothy

Lewis, Rt. Rev. William F., Episcopal Bishop of Olympia

Linder, Hon. Harold F. (CFR)

Linen, James A., Publisher, Time Magazine

Linton, M. Albert, Retired Chairman of the Board, Provident Mutual Life Insurance Company of Philadelphia; Member, American Friends Service Committee

Lipsky, Dr. George A.

Litchfield, Dr. Edward H. (CFR)

Little, Dr. Clarence C., Professor Emeritus, Harvard University and University of Michigan

Littlejohn, Edward

Lockmiller, Dr. David A., President, Ohio Wesleyan University; Former President, University of Chattanooga

Loehr, Rev. Clement D.

Loehr, Rev. Franklin D.

Louchheim, Stuart F.

Louis, Karl N.

Loveless, Herschel C., Governor of Iowa

Loynd, H. J., President, Parke, Davis & Co.

Lubin, Isador (CFR)

Luce, Hon. Clare Boothe, Former Ambassador to Italy; Playwright (Husband in CFR)

Luce, Henry III (CFR)

Lucey, Most Rev. Robert E., S.T.D., Archbishop of San Antonio; Vice President, Catholic Association for International Peace

Lund, Dr. P. Edward

Lunsford, Frank

Mabey, Charles R., Former Governor of Utah

MacLachlan, James A., Professor of Law, Harvard University

Malott, Dr. Deane W., President, Cornell University

Mann, Gerald C., Former Secretary of State for Texas; Former Attorney General, State of Texas; Chairman of the Board, Diversa, Inc., Dallas; Secretary, Board of Trustees; Southern Methodist University

Marlowe, Mark V.

Marshall, Gen. George C., Former Secretary of State; Former Secretary of Defense

Marshall, Brig. Gen. S. L. A., Chief Editorial Writer, Detroit News

Martie, J. E., Past National Vice Commander, American Legion

Martin, Dr. B. Joseph, President, Wesleyan College, Macon, Georgia

Martin, Laurance C.

Marts, Dr. Arnaud C. (CFR)

Mather, Dr. J. Paul, President, University of Massachusetts

Mather, Wiley W.

Mathews, Lt. Col. John A.

Mathieu, Miss Beatrice

Matthews, Allan F.

McAllister, Mrs. Dorothy

McAshan, Mrs. S. M.

McCain, Dr. James A., President, Kansas State College; Former President, Montana State University

McCall, Dr. Duke, President, Southern Baptist Theological Seminary

McCalmont, David B.

McCann, Dr. Kevin, President, Defiance College, Ohio; Special Assistant and speech writer for President Eisenhower, 1955-61

McCarthy, Frank, Producer, Twentieth Century-Fox Films; Former Assistant Secretary of State; Secretary to General George C. Marshall, 1941-1945

McCord, Dr. James I., President, Princeton Theological Seminary

McCormick, Charles T., Distinguished Professor of Law, University of Texas; Former Dean of School of Law, University of North Carolina; Former Professor of Law, Northwestern University

McCormick, Leo H.

McCrady, Dr. Edward, President, University of the South

McDonald, David J., President, United Steelworkers of America

McDonald, Rt. Rev. Msgr. William J., Rector, Catholic University of America.

McFarland, Mrs. Cole

McFee, William

McIntosh, Henry T.

McInturff, George L.

McKee, Frederick C. (CFR)

McKeldin, Theodore R., Former Governor of Maryland

McKinney, Robert, Publisher & Editor, Santa Fe New Mexican; Former Assistant Secretary of the Interior

McLane, John R., Retired Chairman, New Hampshire State Board of Arbitration and Conciliation; Trustee, Dartmouth College

McMath, Sidney S., Former Governor of Arkansas

McMullen, Mrs. Stewart Y.

McNaughton, F. F.

McNaughton, William F.

McNichols, Stephen L. R., Governor of Colorado

McQuarrie, Mrs. Irvine

Means, Paul B., Chairman, Department of Religion, University of Oregon

Meeman, Edward J., Editor, Memphis Press-Scimitar

Melvin, Crandall, Partner, Melvin & Melvin, Lawyers; President, Merchants National Bank & Trust Company, Syracuse; Trustee, Syracuse University; Member, National Council, Boy Scouts of America

Menuhin, Yehudi, Concert Violinist and Symphony Conductor

Merriam, H. G.

Mesta, Perle, Former Minister to Luxembourg

Meyer, Maj. Gen. G. Ralph

Meyner, Robert B., Governor of New Jersey

Mickle, Dr. Joe J., President, Centenary College, Louisiana; Member, Foreign Policy Association; Recipient, Distinguished Alumnis Award, Southern Methodist University, 1953

Midgley, Grant W.

Miller, Dr. Arthur L., Past Moderator, United Presbyterian Church, USA; member, General Board, National Council of Churches

Miller, Francis P. (CFR)

Miller, Harlan, Columnist, Des Moines Register & Tribune

274

Miller, Perry, Professor of American Literature, Harvard University

Miller, Mrs. Walter I.

Milligan, Mrs. Harold, Past President, National Council of Women

Millikan, Dr. Clark B. (CFR)

Millikan, Dr. Max (CFR)

Millis, Dr. John S. (CFR)

Mitchell, Don G. (CFR)

Moehlman, W. F.

Moll, Dr. Lloyd A.

Monroe, J. Raburn, Partner, Monroe & Lemann, Lawyers, New Orleans; Regional Vice President, National Municipal Association

Montgomery, Greenville D.

Montgomery, Dr. John C.

Montgomery, Dr. Riley B., President, College of the Bible, Lexington, Kentucky; Official, National Council of Churches; Member, Fellowship of Reconciliation, World Fellowship, National Education Association, National Council of Churches; Former Chairman, Committee on Activities, Virginia Council of Churches; Former member Executive Committee, Federal Council of Churches

Montgomery, Victor P.

Mooney, James D. (CFR)

Moor, N. R. H.

Moore, Bishop Arthur J., President, Board of Missions and Church Extension, Methodist Church

Moore, Hugh (CFR)

Moore, Rev. Philip S.

Moore, Walden

Morgan, Dr. Arthur E., Former President, Antioch College; Former Head, TVA

Morgenthau, Dr. Hans J. (CFR)

Morrison, deLesseps S., U. S. Ambassador to the Organization of American States; Mayor of New Orleans, 1946-1961

Morse, Samuel F. B., Realtor, San Francisco

Mueller, Bishop Reuben H., Vice-President, National Council of Churches; President, Board of Bishops, United Brethren Church; Vice Chairman, World Council of Christian Education; Official, World Council of Churches

Muir, Malcolm (CFR)

Mullins, Dr. David W., President, University of Arkansas; Member National Council, National Planning Association; Official, National Education Association

Murphy, Dr. Franklin D. (CFR)

Mynders, Alfred D.

Nason, Dr. John W. (CFR)

Nelson, Hon. Gaylord A., Governor of Wisconsin

Neuberger, Richard L., Senator from Oregon; Official, American for Democratic Action

Newman, Dr. James H., Executive Vice President, University of Alabama

Newstetter, Wilbur I., Jr.

Nichols, Rt. Rev. Shirley H., Episcopal Bishop of Kansas

Nichols, Thomas S. (CFR)

Noble, Rev. Charles C., Dean, Chapel of Syracuse University

Noelte, Albert E.

Northrop, Dr. Filmer S. C., Sterling Professor of Philosophy and Law, Yale University; Author

Norton, Hon. Garrison, President, Institute for Defense Analyses; Assistant Secretary of the Navy, 1956-59; Assistant Secretary of State, 1947-49

Norton, Mrs. H. W.

Norton, R. W., Jr.

Nutting, Charles B., President, Action-Housing, Inc.; Former Vice Chancellor, University of Pittsburgh; Former Professor of Law, University of Nebraska

Nuveen, John (CFR)

Odegard, Dr. Peter, Professor of Political Science, University of California; Member, Foreign Policy Association, Former Official, Ford Foundation

Oldham, Rt. Rev. G. Ashton

O'Neal, F. Hodge, Professor of Law, Duke University

Oppenheimer, Dr. J. Robert (CFR)

Oppenheimer, William H., Lawyer, St. Paul, Minnesota

Orgill, Hon. Edmund, Former Mayor of Memphis

Orgill, Joseph, Jr.

Ormond, Dr. John K., Surgeon, Pontiac, Michigan

Orr, Edgar K.

Osborn, Mrs. Chase S., Author, Sault Ste. Marie, Michigan

Osborne, Hon. Lithgow (CFR)

Osgood, William B.

Otenasek, Dr. Mildred

Otis, Courtlandt

Owens, Lee E., Official, Owens Publications, California

Owens, Lee E., Jr.

Pack, Rev. John Paul

Palmer, Charles Forrest, President, Palmer, Inc., Realtor, Atlanta; Official, National Planning Association; Member, Foreign Policy Association, American Society of Planning Officials

Palmer, Miss Hazel, Past President, National Federation of Business and Professional Women's Clubs

Palmer, Robert C.

Parker, Haven

Parker, Mrs. Kay Peterson

Parran, Dr. Thomas, President, Avalon Foundation; Former Surgeon General, U.S.; Former Dean, Graduate School of Public Health, University of Pittsburgh

Parran, Mrs. Thomas

Partch, Mrs. Wallace

Pasqualicchio, Leonard H., President, National Council of American-Italian Friendship

Patten, James G., President, National Farmers' Union; President, International Federation of Agricultural Producers; Trustee, National Planning Association

Patty, Dr. Ernest N., President, University of Alaska

Pavlo, Mrs. Hattie May

Pearl, Stuart D.

Peattie, Donald Culross, Author, Roving Editor, Reader's Digest

Pell, Herbert Claiborne, Former Congressman from New York; Member, Advertising Council, Rhode Island Labor Department; Member, Advisory Council, Yenching University, Peiping, China

Pell, Rev. Walden, II

Perkins, Dr. John A., President, University of Delaware; Undersecretary of Health, Education & Welfare, 1957-58; Director, International City Managers Association; Member, Committee for Economic Development; Member National Planning Association

Perkins, Ralph

Phillips, Duncan, Director, Phillips Gallery, Washington, D. C.

Phillips, Dr. Hubert

Phillips, Dr. J. Donald, President, Hillsdale College, Michigan

Phillips, William (CFR)

Pillsbury, Philip W., Chairman of the Board, Pillsbury Mills, Inc.

Pillsbury, Mrs. Philip W.

Pines, Rabbi Jerome M.

Pinkerton, Roy D., President & Editorial Director, John P. Scripps Newspapers

Pond, Harold S.

Pool, Rev. Dr. D. deSola (CFR)

Popejoy, Dr. Tom L., President, University of New Mexico

Porter, Paul A., Former Chairman, Federal Communications Commission

Posner, Stanley I., Professor of Business Administration, American University, Washington, D. C.

Prange, Charles H., President, Austenal, Inc.

Price, Gwilym A., Chairman, Westinghouse Electric Corporation; Member, Business Advisory Council

Prickett, William, Lawyer, Wilmington, Delaware

Puffer, Dr. Claude E., Vice Chancellor, University of Buffalo; Member, Committee for Economic Development

Qualls, J. Winfield

Quay, Richard R.

Quimby, Thomas H. E., Democratic National Committeeman for Michigan; Vice President, Perry Land Company

Quinn, William Francis, Governor of Hawaii

Raasch, John E., Chairman of Board, John Wanamaker

Rabb, Maxwell M., Partner, Stroock, Stroock & Lavan, New York City; Secretary to the Cabinet of the U. S., 1953-58; Former Chairman, Government Division, United Jewish Appeal; Consultant, Secretary of the Navy, 1946; Administrative Assistant to Senator Henry Cabot Lodge, 1937-43; Administrative Assistant to Senator Sinclair Weeks, 1944

Radley, Guy R.

Raines, Bishop Richard C., Indiana Area, Methodist Church

Rainey, Dr. Homer P., Former President, University of Texas, Stephens College, Bucknell University; Liberal-Loyalist Democratic Candidate for Governor of Texas, 1946

Raley, Dr. John Wesley, President, Oklahoma Baptist University

Rasmuson, Elmer E., President, National Bank of Alaska

Redd, Charles

Reed, Alexander P., Chairman of the Board, Fidelity Trust Company, Pittsburgh

Reed, Dr. R. Glenn, Jr.

Reese, Dr. Curtis W., Editor, Unity; Member, Council of Liberal Churches

Reeves, Dr. George N.

Remsen, Gerard T.

Renne, Dr. Roland R., President, Montana State College

Rettaliata, Dr. John T., President, Illinois Institute of Technology

Reuther, Victor G., Administrative Assistant to the President, United Automobile Workers

Reuther, Walter P., President, United Automobile Workers; President, CIO Division, AFL-CIO; Vice President, United World Federalists

Rhodes, Dr. Peyton N., President, Southwestern University, Memphis

Rhyne, Charles S., Past President, American Bar Association; Member, Executive Council, American Society for International Law

Rice, Dr. Allan Lake

Rice, Dr. Warner G., Chairman, Department of English, University of Michigan

Roberts, David W.

Roberts, Mrs. Owen J.

Robertson, Andrew W. (CFR)

Robertson, Walter S., Former Assistant Secretary of State for far Eastern Affairs; former delegate to U. N.

Robinson, Claude W.

Robinson, Miss Elizabeth

Robinson, J. Ben

Robinson, John Q.

Robinson, Thomas L. (CFR)

Roebling, Mrs. Mary G., President & Chairman of Board, Trenton Trust Company

Rogers, Will, Jr., Newspaper Publisher, Former Congressman

Rolph, Thomas W.

Roosevelt, Nicholas (CFR)

Roper, Elmo (CFR)

Rose, Dr. Frank A., President, University of Alabama

Rosenthal, Milton F., President, Hugo Stinnes Corp.

Rostow, Dr. Eugene V. (CFR)

Rowland, W. T.

Rudick, Harry J., Partner, Lord, Day & Lord; Professor of Law New York University; Member, Committee for Economic Development, National Planning Association

Rust, Ben

Ruthenburg, Louis, Chairman of Board, Servel, Inc.

Ryder, Melvin, Publisher, Editor, President, Army Times Publishing Company

Sagendorph, Robb, Publisher, Old Farmer's Almanack

Sandelius, Walter E.

Sanders, Walter B., Chairman, Department of Architecture, University of Michigan

Sanford, Arthur

Sayman, Mrs. Thomas

Sayre, Francis B., Assistant Secretary of State, 1933-39; U. S. Ambassador to the United Nations, 1947-52; Professor of Law, Harvard University, 1917-34

Scherman, Harry (CFR)

Schiff, Mrs. Dorothy, Publisher and owner, New York Post

Schlesinger, Dr. Arthur, Jr. (CFR)

Schmidt, Adolph W. (CFR)

Schmidt, John F.

Schmitt, Mrs. Ralph S.

Schroeder, Walter, President, Christian Schroeder & Sons Inc., Milwaukee

Schroth, Thomas N., Editor & Publisher, Congressional Quarterly, Inc.

Schultz, Larry H.

Scullin, Richard J., Jr.

Seedorf, Dr. Evelyn H.

Semmes, Brig Gen. Harry H.

Sengstacke, John H., Publisher, Chicago Defender

Serpell, Mrs. John A.

Shackelford, Francis, Lawyer, Atlanta; Assistant Secretary of the Army, 1952-53

Shapiro, Ascher H., Professor of Engineering, Massachusetts Institute of Technology

Shea, George E., Jr., Financial Editor, Wall Street Journal

Shelton, E. G.

Shepley, Dr. Ethan A. H., Chancellor, Washington University, St. Louis; Board member, Southwestern Bell Telephone Company, Anheuser-Busch, Inc.

Sherman, Dr. Mary S.

Sherwood, Carlton M., President, Pierce, Hedrick & Sherwood, Inc.; Member, Executive Committee, Foundation for Integrated Education; Commission member, National Council of Churches

Shirpser, Mrs. Clara

Shotwell, Dr. James T. (CFR)

Sibley, Brig. Gen. Alden K.

Sick, Emil G., Chairman of the Board, Sicks' Breweries, Ltd.; President, Washmont Corp., Sicks' Breweries Enterprises, Inc.

Sikes, W. E.

Simons, Dolph, President, The World Company; Publisher, Editor, Lawrence, Kansas Daily Journal-World; Director, Associated Press

Simonton, Theodore E.

Simpson, James A., Lawyer, Birmingham, Alabama; Former State Senator

Sittler, Edward L., Jr.

Skouras, Spyros P., President, Twentieth Century-Fox Film Corp.; President of Skouras Lines

Slee, James N.

Slick, Tom, Chairman of the Board, Slick Oil Company; Board Member, Slick Airways, Inc., Dresser Industries of Dallas

Sloan, Rev. Harold P., Jr.

Slosson, Dr. Preston W., Professor of History, University of Michigan; Author

Sly, Rev. Virgil A., Vice-President, National Council of Churches, Official, World Council of Churches

Smith, Bishop A. Frank, Chairman of the Board of Trustees, Southern Methodist University, Dallas; Methodist Bishop of Houston and San Antonio

Smith, Maj. Gen. Edward S., Former Vice-President, Southern Bell T & T Company

Smith, Dr. Francis A.

Smith, H. Alexander (CFR)

Smith, Paul C. (CFR)

Smith, Robert Jerome

Smith, Russell G.

Smith, Dr. Seymour A., President, Stephens College

Smith, Sylvester C., Jr., Lawyer, Newark, New Jersey

Snow, Miss Jessie L.

Snyder, John I., Jr., Chairman of the Board, President, U. S. Industries, Inc.; Formerly with Kuhn, Loeb & Co.; Trustee Committee for Economic Development, National Urban League, New York University

Soffel, Judge Sara M., Judge, Court of Common Pleas, Allegheny County, Pennsylvania; Trustee, University of Pittsburgh; Official, National Conference of Christians and Jews

Sommer, Mrs. Sara

Sonne, Hans Christian (CFR)

Spaulding, Rev. Clarence

Spaulding, Eugene R., Vice-President, The New Yorker

Spaulding, George F.

Spilsbury, Mrs. Margaret C.

Spivak, Lawrence E., Producer, "Meet the Press," NBC-TV; Former Editor & Publisher, American Mercury

Sporn, Philip, President, American Electric Power Company & subsidiaries

Springer, Maurice

Sproul, Dr. Robert Gordon (CFR)

Stafford, Mrs. Carl

Standley, Rear Adm. William H. (CFR)

Stanton, Dr. Frank, President, Columbia Broadcasting System; Member, Business Advisory Council

Starcher, Dr. George W., President, University of North Dakota

Stark, George W., Arthur, Columnist, Detroit News

Steinbicker, Dr. Paul G., Chairman, Department of Government, St. Louis University

Steiner, Dr. Celestin John, S. J., President, University of Detroit; Member, Foreign Policy Association; Member, National Conference of Christians and Jews

Steinkraus, Herman W., Chairman of the Board, Bridgeport Brass Co.; Former President, U. S. Chamber of Commerce; Trustee, Twentieth Century Fund

Steinman, Dr. David B., Bridge Engineer

Stern, William

Sterne, Dr. Theodore E., Simon Newcomb Professor of Astrophysics, Harvard University

Stevenson, Adlai (CFR)

Stevenson, Dr. William E. (CFR)

Steward, Roy F.

Stewart, Dr. Robert B. (CFR)

Stoddard, Ralph

Stoke, Dr. Harold Walter, President, Queens College, Flushing, New York; Former President, Louisiana State University

Straus, Ralph I. (CFR)

Strausz-Hupe, Dr. Robert (CFR)

Streit, Clarence K., President, Federal Union, Inc.; Author

Stuart, Dr. Graham H.

Sturt, Dr. Daniel W.

Suits, Hollis E.

Talbott, Philip M., Past President, U. S. Chamber of Commerce

Tally, Joseph, Jr., Past President, Kiwanis International

Tatum, Lofton L.

Tawes, J. Millard, Governor of Maryland

Taylor, Dr. Edgar Curtis

Taylor, James L.

Taylor, Gen. Maxwell D. (CFR)

Taylor, Brig. Gen. Telford, U. S. Chief of Consul, Nurnburg War Criminals Trials

Taylor, Dr. Theophilus Mills, Moderator, United Presbyterian Church, USA; Official, World Council of Churches

Taylor, Wayne Chatfield (CFR)

Teller, Dr. Edward (CFR)

Thom, W. Taylor, Jr., Chairman Emeritus of Geological Engineering, Princeton University

Thomas, J. R.

Thompson, Dr. Ernest Trice, Professor, Union Theological Seminary; Co-Editor, Presbyterian Outlook

Thompson, Kelly, President, Western Kentucky State College

Tobie, Llewellyn A.

Todd, Dr. G. W.

Todd, George L., Vice President, Burroughs Corp.

Tolan, Mrs. Thomas L.

Towill, John Bell

Towster, Julian

Trickett, Dr. A. Stanley, Chairman, Department of History, University of Omaha; Official, World Council of Churches

Truman, Harry S., Former President of the United States

Turner, Gardner C.

Turner, Jennie M.

Twiss, Rev. Malcolm N.

Upgren, Dr. Arthur R. (CFR)

Urey, Dr. Harold C., Nobel Prize Atomic Chemist; Professor of Chemistry, University of California; Former Professor of Chemistry, University of Chicago

Valimont, Col. R. W.

Van Doren, Mark, Pulitzer Prize Poet

van Nierop, H. A.

Van Zandt, J. Parker

Veiller, Anthony

Velte, Charles H.

Vereide, Abraham, President, International Christian Leadership

Vernon, Lester B.

Vieg, Dr. John A.

Vincent, John H.

Visson, Andre

Walker, Elmer

Walker, Dr. Harold Blake, President, McCormick Theological Seminary, Evanston, Illinois

Walling, L. Metcalfe, Director, U. S. Operations Mission, Colombia; Vice President, National Consumers League

Walsh, John R.

Walsh, Dr. Warren B., Chairman of the Board, Department of Russian Studies, Syracuse University; Director, American Unitarian Association

Walton, Miss Dorothy C.

Wampler, Cloud, Chairman of Board, Carrier Corporation

Wanger, Walter F. (CFR)

Wansker, Harry A.

Warner, Dr. Sam B., Publisher, Shore Line Times, The Clinton

Warren, Hamilton M.

Warwick, Dr. Sherwood

Waterman, Professor Leroy

Watkins, Bishop William T., Methodist Bishop of Louisville, Kentucky

Watts, Olin E., Member, Jennings, Watts, Clarke & Hamilton, Lawyers; Jacksonville, Florida; Trustee, University of Florida

Waymack, William Wesley, Former member, Atomic Energy Commission; Former Editor, Des Moines Register & Tribune; Pulitzer Prize, 1937; Member, National Committee, American Civil Liberties Union; Trustee, Twentieth Century Fund

Webb, Marshall

Webb, Vanderbilt (CFR)

Wedel, Mrs. Theodore O., Past President, United Church Women

Weeks, Dr. I. D., President, University of South Dakota

Welch, Mrs. George Patrick

Wells, Dr. Herman B. (CFR)

Weltner, Dr. Philip

Wendover, Sanford H.

West, Donald C.

Weston, Eugene, Jr., Architect, Los Angeles; Member, American Society of Planning Officials

Weston, Rev. Robert G.

Wetmore, Rev. Canon J. Stuart

Whitaker, Robert B.

White, Edward S.

White, Dr. Lee A., Retired Editorial Writer, Detroit News

White, William L., Publisher, Emporia, Kansas Gazette; Author; Member, Former Director, American Civil Liberties Union

White, Dr. W. R., President, Baylor University, Waco, Texas

Whitman, Walter G., Chairman. Department of Chemical Engineering, Massachusetts Institute of Technology; Secretary-General, United Nations Conference on Peaceful Use of Atomic Energy, 1955

Whitney, Edward Allen

Whorf, Richard, Producer, Actor, Director, Warner Brothers; Producer, CBS, Hollywood

Wiesner, Dr. Jerome B. (CFR)

Wigner, Dr. Eugene P., Professor, Princeton University

Wilkin, Robert N.

Willham, Dr. Oliver S., President, Oklahoma State University

Williams, A. N., Former Chairman of Board, Westinghouse Air Brake Company

Williams, Dr. Clanton W., President, University of Houston

Williams, Herbert H.

Williams, Mrs. Lynn A., Sr.

Williams, Ray G.

Williams, Whiting

Williamson, Alexander J.

Willkie, Philip, Son of Wendell Willkie

Wilson, Alfred M., Vice President, Director, Minneapolis-Honeywell Regulator Company

Wilson, Dr. Logan, President, University of Texas; Director, Center of Advanced Study in Behavioral Sciences; Former member, Fund for the Republic

Wilson, Dr. O. Meredith, President, University of Minnesota

Wise, Watson W., Owner, W. W. Wise Drilling, Inc., Tyler, Texas; Member, Executive Committee, Lone Star Steel Co.; Dallas; Special Council, Schuman Plan, NATO, 1949-52; Member, National Planning Association; U. S. Delegate, 13th General Assembly of the United Nations

Woodring, Harry H., Former Secretary of War; Past National Commander, American Legion

Wright, William

Yarnell, Rear Adm. H. E. (CFR)

Young, John L., Vice-President, U. S. Steel Corporation; Chairman of the Board, Dad's Root Beer Bottling Company; Member, Foreign Policy Association

Young, John Orr, Advertising Consultant, New York City

Young, Owen D. (CFR)

Youngdahl, Luther W., Judge, U. S. District Court for District of Columbia; Former Governor of Minnesota; Trustee, American University

Zanuck, Darryl F., Vice-President, Twentieth Century-Fox Film Corp.

Zellerbach, Harold L., Former Board Chairman, Crown Zellerbach Corp.; Member, Board of Governors, Hebrew Union College; Trustee, University of Pennsylvania

9 781374 837621